DIGITAL INNOVATION FOR SMARTER CLIMATE ACTION

Asia-Pacific Digital Transformation Report 2024

United Nations publication
Sales no: E.24.II.F.10
Copyright © United Nations 2024
All rights reserved
PRINT ISBN: 9789210032346
PDF ISBN: 9789211066616

Photo credits:
Page 1: Getty Images
Page 6: Chuttersnap/Unsplash
Page 16: Alexei Marchenko/Unsplash
Page 47: Denys Nevochai/Unsplash
Page 57: Hartano Creative Studio

Foreword

In Asia and the Pacific, the climate crisis intersects with digital transformations through a complex mix of challenges and opportunities, creating a series of vicious but also potentially virtuous cycles. The *Asia-Pacific Digital Transformation Report 2024* considers how digital transformations will structurally and irreversibly affect the trajectory of climate change. It presents a digital-growth-climate nexus to better understand the diverse and dynamic picture and considers ways in which the region can follow the most positive trajectory to avert a climate catastrophe.

The *Report* presents 27 cases demonstrating the power of digital applications for climate actions – across infrastructure, governance, mobility, industry and trade, disaster risk reduction, agriculture and biodiversity ecosystems. These examples underscore the notion that digital innovations have enabled more sophisticated climate mitigation measures, contributing to both decarbonization and dematerialization. There exists a positive correlation between digital transformations and energy transition, indicating that a country's readiness to transition to sustainable energy practices is influenced by its digital capabilities. Notably, digitalization is enabling all infrastructures to become steadily smarter, enhancing efficiencies in energy consumption and supply and facilitating the integration of renewables throughout the lifecycle of infrastructure from the design, construction, operation and management stages to reusing infrastructure waste. Furthermore, artificial intelligence-driven geospatial data analytics is contributing to climate adaptation by improving the accuracy and timeliness of early warning systems.

Asia and the Pacific, as a hub for digitally driven innovations, should continue leveraging these advancements to achieve Sustainable Development Goal 13 on climate action. The Asia-Pacific Ministerial Conference on Digital Inclusion and Transformation, hosted by the Government of Kazakhstan from 3 to 5 September 2024, presents an opportune moment to commit to a vision that harnesses the full potential of digital solutions and scales up adoption through regional cooperation. We hope this report sets the stage for productive discussions and inspires deliberate policy actions at local, national and regional levels on maximizing opportunities for sustainable development and addressing climate risks.

Armida Salsiah Alisjahbana
Under-Secretary-General of the United Nations and Executive Secretary of ESCAP

Acknowledgements

The *Asia-Pacific Digital Transformation Report 2024* is a biennial flagship publication of the United Nations Economic and Social Commission for Asia and the Pacific (ESCAP). This second edition was prepared under the leadership and guidance of Armida Salsiah Alisjahbana, Under-Secretary-General of the United Nations and Executive Secretary of ESCAP. Lin Yang, Deputy Executive Secretary, supported by ESCAP's Editorial Board, and Tiziana Bonapace, Director of the ICT and Disaster Risk Reduction Division, provided direction and advice.

This report was prepared by a core drafting team led by Tae Hyung Kim, Chief of the ICT and Development Section, including consultants Seunghwa Jun, Jongsur Park, and Charlene Lui. Substantive contributions were provided by staff members of the ICT and Development Section: Siope Vakataki 'Ofa, Daesik Shin, Sowi Kim, Aida Karazhanova, and Lingling Zhang; as well as consultants Rony Medaglia and Seul Ki Yi.

The contributors of ESCAP divisions include Hamid Mehmood and Chul Min Lee of the Space Applications Section, and Sanjay Srivastava, Madhurima Sarkar-Swaisgood, Rahul Kumar Suman, and Temily Isabella Baker of the Disaster Risk Reduction Section, ICT and Disaster Risk Reduction Division; and Yann Duval and Tientip Subhanij of the Trade, Investment and Innovation Division.

The contributors and reviewers from external partner organizations include: Michel Bergeron, Katharine Ghidella, Cynthia Primo Bou, and Shamina de Gonzaga of the United Nations Global Service Centre; Woojin Han and Valentin Rudloff of the United Nations Climate Technology Centre & Network; Yeonjoo Bang, Hyogeon Lee, Joonyong Park, and Jaesung Park of the Korea Minting, Security Printing & ID Card Operating Corporation; Kenddrick Chan of the Tony Blair Institute for Global Change; Leila Guici of GSMA; Duk Jo Kong of the Gwangju Institute of Science and Technology of Korea; and Huawei.

Peter Stalker provided substantive editing, and Anoushka Ali copyedited the report. Daniel Feary designed the layout and graphics. Administrative assistance was provided by Tarnkamon Chantarawat, Pradtana Limkrailassiri, Narathit Sirirat and Yukhontorn Suewaja of the ICT and Disaster Risk Reduction Division. Support was provided by the interns in the ICT and Disaster Risk Reduction Division: Swapnil Vashishtha, Venkatesh Aruldoss, Seolhee Jeon, Dominic Pollatat Wiesmann, Elisa Belaz, and Christal Cheng.

The ESCAP Communications and Knowledge Management Section coordinated the media launch and report outreach.

Contents

Boxes

Figures

Tables

Abbreviations

AI	artificial intelligence
ASEAN	Association of Southeast Asian Nations
CO$_2$	carbon dioxide
DTI	Digital Transformation Index
ESCAP	Economic and Social Commission for Asia and the Pacific
GDP	gross domestic product
GHG	greenhouse gas
GPS	Global Positioning System
GtCO$_2$e	gigatons of carbon dioxide equivalent
GW	gigawatt
GWh	gigawatt-hour
ETI	Energy Transition Index
IEA	International Energy Agency
IoT	Internet of Things
kWh	kilowatt-hour
MTCO$_2$e	Metric tons of carbon dioxide equivalent
MWh	megawatt-hour
SDG	Sustainable Development Goals
TWh	terawatt-hour
UNCTCN	United Nations Climate Technology Centre and Network
UNEP	United Nations Environment Programme
UNGSC	United Nations Global Service Centre

Executive Summary

Digital big bang in a climate crisis

The Asia-Pacific region contributes to over half of the world's total greenhouse gas (GHG) emissions (ESCAP, 2022b). However, the region is also highly vulnerable to the consequences of a climate catastrophe, notably through more frequent extreme weather events and other disasters, with average annual losses increasing from $924 billion to almost $1 trillion (ESCAP, 2023a). The region is diverse, with some of the top carbon emitters in the world alongside smaller emitters, who are also the most vulnerable and exposed to the impacts of climate change (ESCAP, and others, 2023).

At the same time, countries in Asia and the Pacific are at the heart of digital transformations. In the context of this *Report*, the term digital transformation goes beyond the digitalization of goods and services. It represents a new development paradigm, reweaving the whole fabric of society, in terms of value creation, management, use and distribution through applications of disruptive technologies, including artificial intelligence (AI), digital data, connectivity and networks (ESCAP, 2022a).

New digital devices and platforms can help tackle the climate crisis and reduce long-term energy consumption, but this needs to be considered against the immediate impact of these devices on electricity consumption. Given the region's continued reliance on non-renewable energy resources, rising electricity demand in the near-term results in more greenhouse gases emitted into the atmosphere.

In Asia and the Pacific, the climate crisis intersects with digital transformations through a complex mix of challenges and opportunities, creating a series of vicious but also potentially virtuous cycles. The *Asia-Pacific Digital Transformation Report 2024* considers how digital transformations will structurally and irreversibly impact the trajectory of climate change. The report presents a digital-growth-climate nexus to better understand the diverse and dynamic picture and considers the ways in which the Asia-Pacific region can follow the most positive trajectory to avert a climate catastrophe.

The digital-growth-climate nexus

Today's digital transformations are the latest chapter in the story of industrialization, productivity, economic growth and social changes. Historically, economic growth has led to greater environmental degradation; as countries industrialize, they generally become more productive, yet generate more greenhouse gas emissions. At later stages of development, and with the use of more sophisticated technologies, there is a turning point beyond which the level of carbon emissions tends to fall off.

Digital Transformation Index Framework

This *Report* revisits the Digital Transformation Framework, presented in United Nations Economic and Social Commission for Asia and the Pacific's (ESCAP) *Asia-Pacific Digital Transformation Report 2022: Shaping Our Digital Future* and provides an updated analysis of the Digital Transformation Index (DTI) in the context of climate change.

The Digital Transformation Framework assesses the digital transformation landscape and diagnoses existing digital transformation gaps at the country level, based on three dynamic stages: Foundation, Adoption and Acceleration, and five actors that correspond to five pillars: Infrastructure and Network, Government, Business, People and Ecosystem. Thus, there are 15 separate domains and 105 indicators for tracking the progress of digital transformation.

Digital transformation, economic growth and climate change

In the *Asia-Pacific Digital Transformation Report 2022*, the Digital Transformation Framework showed how more developed countries capitalized on digital capacity and higher economic growth, represented by income level (GDP per capita) (Figure I).

FIGURE I   **The Digital Transformation Index (DTI) Framework**

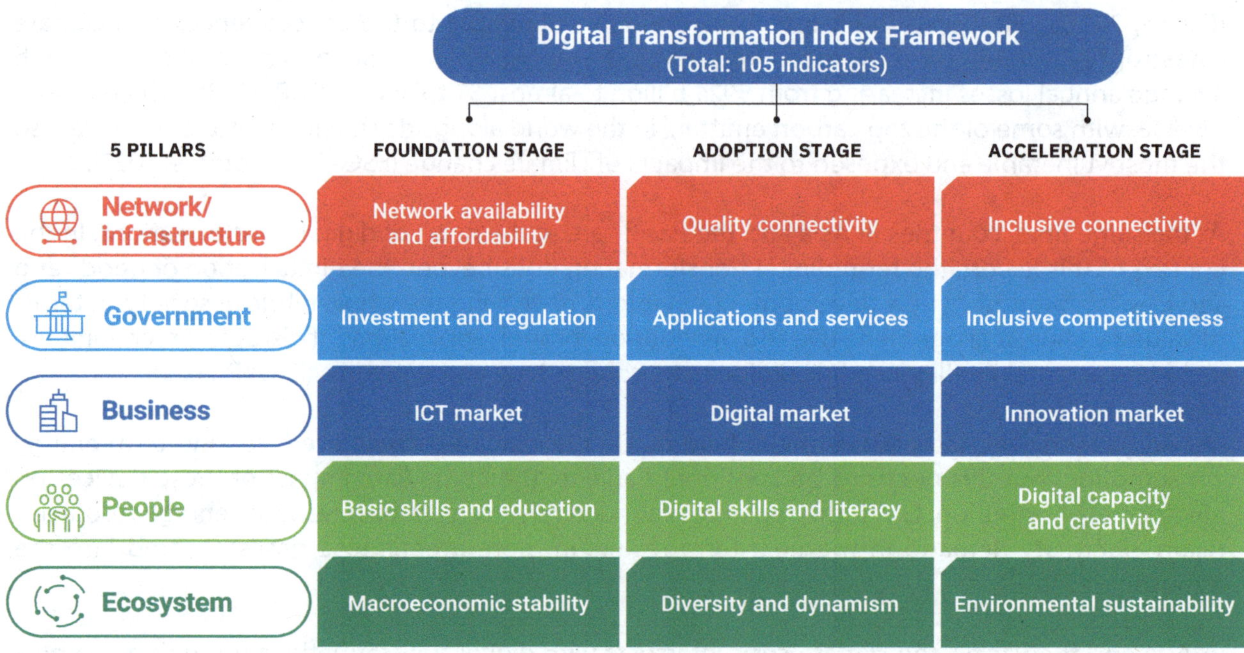

Sources: Elaborated by the authors, based on secondary sources such as Cisco, Economist, Institute for Management Development, Global System for Mobile Communications Association, World Bank, World Economic Forum, World Intellectual Property Organization, etc.

To examine additional parameters in hypothesising the relationship between digital transformation, economic growth and climate change, this *2024 edition* undertakes the following:

Firstly, the *Report* compares carbon emissions change by country[1] from the years 2010 to 2022 with GDP per capita (II-A). Each country for which data are available appears as a dot. Countries above the X-axis generally show both higher incomes and falling emissions. Those in the lower half, generally developing countries, saw an increase in emissions. The analysis finds that, in general, the change starts at a per capita income of between an estimated US$ 14,000 and $20,000, beyond which emissions start to fall. This analysis can also be applied to groups of countries. As shown in Figure II-B, countries in higher income groups saw a greater reduction in carbon emissions.

---

1   In total, 98 countries are included in the analysis, based on the availability of data.

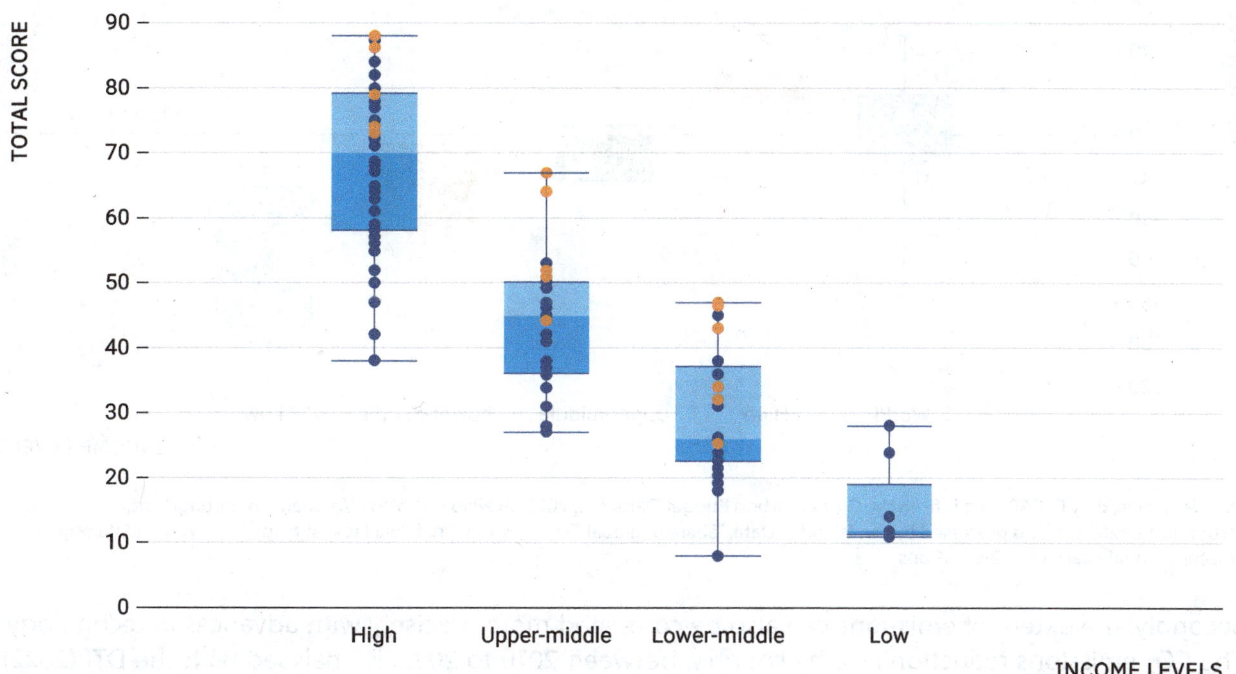

Source: Seunghwa Jun, Jongsur Park, and Jeong Yoon Kim, "Digital transformation landscape in Asia and the Pacific: Aggravated digital divide and widening growth gap", United Nations Economic and Social Commission for Asia and the Pacific (ESCAP), Information and Communications Technology and Disaster Risk Reduction Division, Working Paper Series (Bangkok, July 2022). Available at https://www.unescap.org/kp/2022/ digital-transformation-landscape-asia-and-pacific-aggravated-digital-divide-and-widening

Note: The points show the values of individual countries. The boxes indicate the middle 50 per cent of the data. The box is split at the median value.

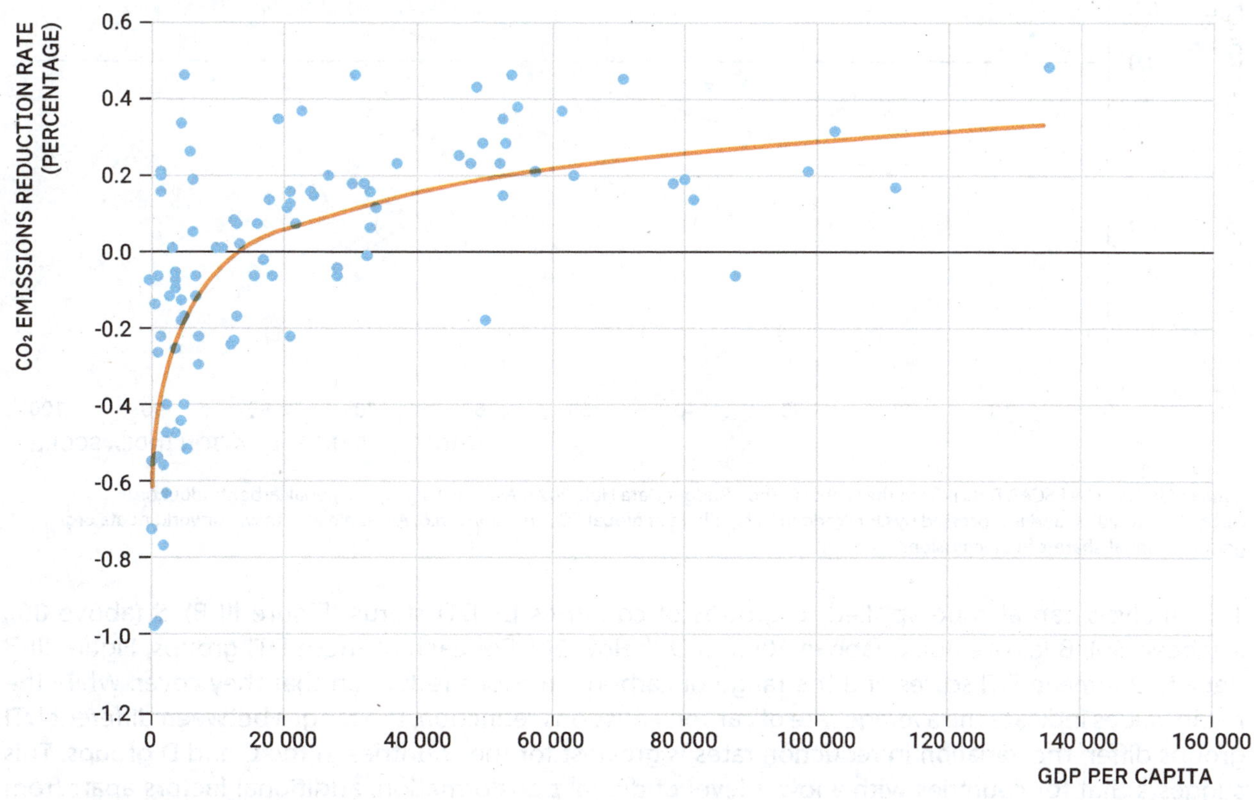

Source: Analysed by ESCAP. Data is from the Global Carbon Budget Data Hub, 2023, and is processed by Our World in Data, "Share of global CO$_2$ emissions", n.d. Available at https://ourworldindata.org/grapher/annual-share-of-co2-emissions

FIGURE II-B   CO$_2$ reduction by income group

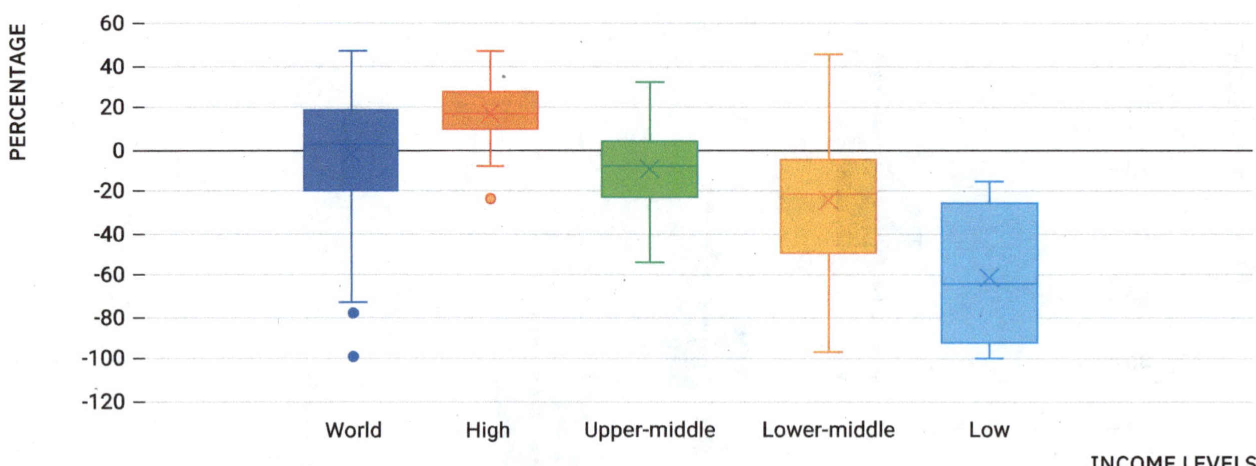

Source: Analysed by ESCAP. Data is from the Global Carbon Budget Data Hub, 2023. Available at https://globalcarbonbudget.org/carbonbudget2023/ and is processed by Our World in Data, "Share of global CO$_2$ emissions", n.d. Available at https://ourworldindata.org/grapher/annual-share-of-co2-emissions

Secondly, the extent of emissions can also be correlated more precisely with advances in technology. The CO$_2$ emissions reduction rate by country, between 2010 to 2022, is analysed with the DTI (2022) (Figure III-A). The DTI takes a value between 0 and 100. With progress in digital transformation, as indicated by a country's DTI score, the extent of CO$_2$ reduction tends to increase. Beyond a DTI score of around 53.12, there is a drop in emissions.

FIGURE III-A   Digital Transformation Index (DTI) and CO$_2$ reduction rate, 2010–2022

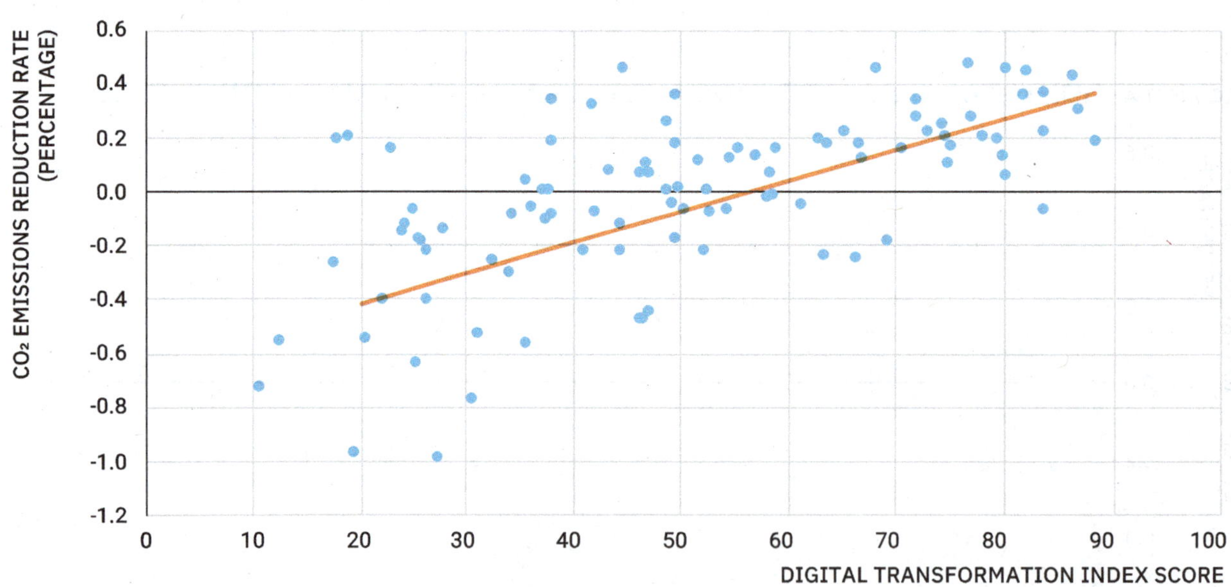

Source: Analysed by ESCAP. Data is from the Global Carbon Budget Data Hub, 2023. Available at https://globalcarbonbudget.org/carbonbudget2023/ and is processed by Our World in Data, "Share of global CO$_2$ emissions", n.d. Available at https://ourworldindata.org/grapher/annual-share-of-co2-emissions

This analysis can also be applied to groups of countries by DTI status (Figure III-B): S (above 80), A (above 60), B (above 40), C (above 20) and D (below 20). For each of these DTI groups, Figure III-B depicts the mean DTI scores and the range of carbon emissions reduction that they cover. While the mean values indicate the average rate of carbon emissions reduction, the ranges between different DTI groups differ; the variation in reduction rates is greatest for the countries in the C and D groups. This suggests that for countries with a lower level of digital transformation, additional factors apart from digital capacities play a significant role, resulting in more uneven progress.

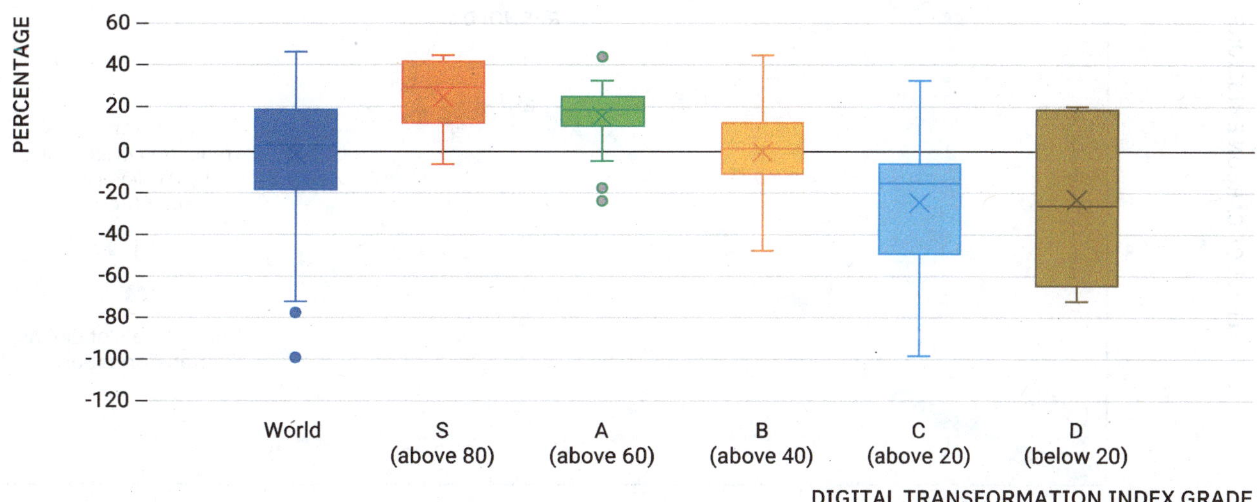

Source: Analysed by ESCAP. Data is from the Global Carbon Budget Data Hub, 2023. Available at https://globalcarbonbudget.org/carbonbudget2023/ and is processed by Our World in Data, "Share of global CO$_2$ emissions", n.d. Available at https://ourworldindata.org/grapher/annual-share-of-co2-emissions

Thirdly, the connections between digital transformation, income and carbon emissions reduction rate are examined further. Table I shows the average CO$_2$ reduction rate for each country income group (high income, upper-middle income and lower-middle income), as well as the average CO$_2$ reduction rate for countries that had the highest DTI scores (S) within that income group. For the high-income countries, the average reduction was 17 per cent, but countries with the highest DTI scores (S) within that group saw a reduction of 26 per cent. This emphasizes that even for countries with similar high incomes, higher digital transformation capacities and capabilities contribute to more effective CO$_2$ reduction.

TABLE I CO$_2$ reduction rate (%) by income group and by high Digital Transformation Index (DTI) score

	HIGH-INCOME COUNTRIES	UPPER-MIDDLE INCOME COUNTRIES	LOWER-MIDDLE INCOME COUNTRIES
Whole group	+17%	-9%	-29%
Countries with higher grade DTI scores in the income group	+26%	-25%	-43%

Source: ESCAP. Data is from the Global Carbon Budget Data Hub, 2023. Available at https://globalcarbonbudget.org/carbonbudget2023/ and is processed by Our World in Data, "Share of global CO$_2$ emissions", n.d. Available at https://ourworldindata.org/grapher/annual-share-of-co2-emissions

On the other hand, for middle- and lower-income countries, progress can be very uneven. Developed countries have undergone digital transformation after industrialization, while developing countries are undergoing digital transformation as they industrialize. In developing countries, structural transformation and other factors can thus outweigh the benefits of digital progress in contributing to CO$_2$ reduction, and by a high margin.

Given the above analysis, Figure IV illustrates the digital-growth-climate nexus schematically. Carbon emissions initially rise with increasing per capita GDP, but beyond a certain threshold, with economic development and technological development, they start to fall, with the reduction likely to be steeper for the countries with the highest digital capacities.

Technological development influences the carbon emissions trajectory, but the extent to which digital technology capacities contribute to climate action will also be conditioned by many other factors, including the country's industrial and economic structures, sociocultural context, and deliberate country policies and actions.

FIGURE IV   **Digital-growth-climate nexus**

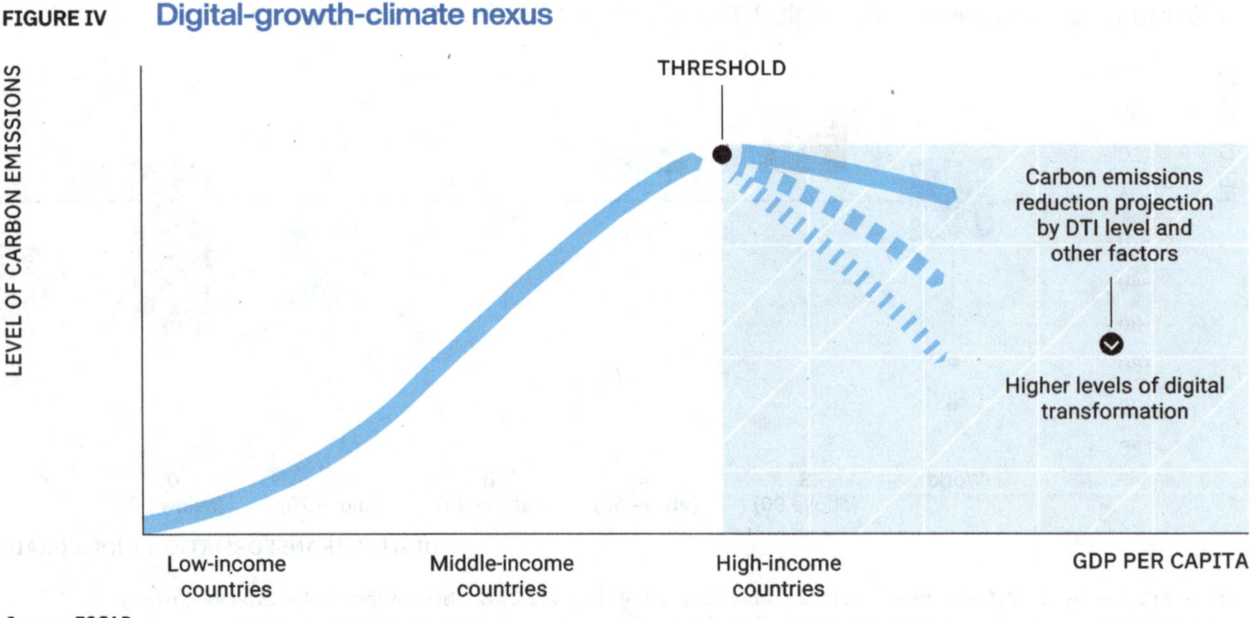

Source: ESCAP.

Digital transformations align with energy transitions

The global energy system is undergoing a notable transformation, with a focus on a just, inclusive and equitable energy transition based on renewables and energy efficiency. In pursuing a reduction of global carbon emissions to net zero by 2050, the transition from fossil fuels to renewable energy is imperative.

Energy transition has important linkages with digital transformation. A higher capacity for digital transformation within a country can potentially indicate its capability to adopt digital tools and solutions for energy optimization, renewables integration, smart grids and energy transition efforts. Conversely, countries that lag in digital transformation may face challenges in fully embracing the opportunities that digitalization offers in the energy sector.

In comparing the Energy Transition Index (ETI)[2] with the Digital Transformation Index to provide a multi-dimensional understanding of a sustainable digital and energy future, this *Report* finds a positive correlation between digital transformations and energy transition readiness. This indicates that a country's readiness to adopt and implement energy transition measures aligns closely with its digital transformation status, emphasizing the influence of digital capabilities on the country's potential to transition towards sustainable energy practices (Figure V-A).

This analysis can also be applied to groups of countries. Figure V-B shows the ETI performance by DTI countries grouped by their DTI status (S/A/B/C/D), and finds that countries with higher levels of digital capacities perform better on the ETI.

The relationship between digital transformation and energy transition is shown to be synergistic, which underlines the importance of using efficient digital infrastructures and systems for energy optimization by integrating renewables and transitioning to greener energy systems, including smart grids with multi-directional power transmission, that can respond to sudden surges in supply or demand and automatically reroute electricity flows.

---

2   World Economic Forum's Energy Transition Index, with two pillars: system performance - current energy system performance; and transition readiness - preparedness and enabling environment for green and smart energy transition.

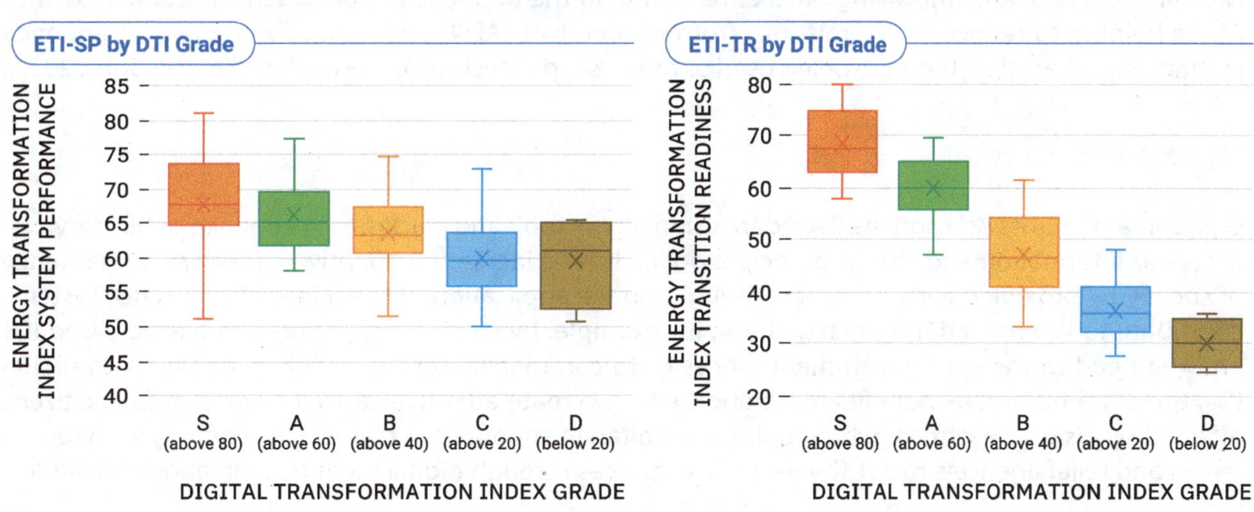

FIGURE V-A Correlations between the Energy Transition Index (ETI) and the Digital Transformation Index (DTI)

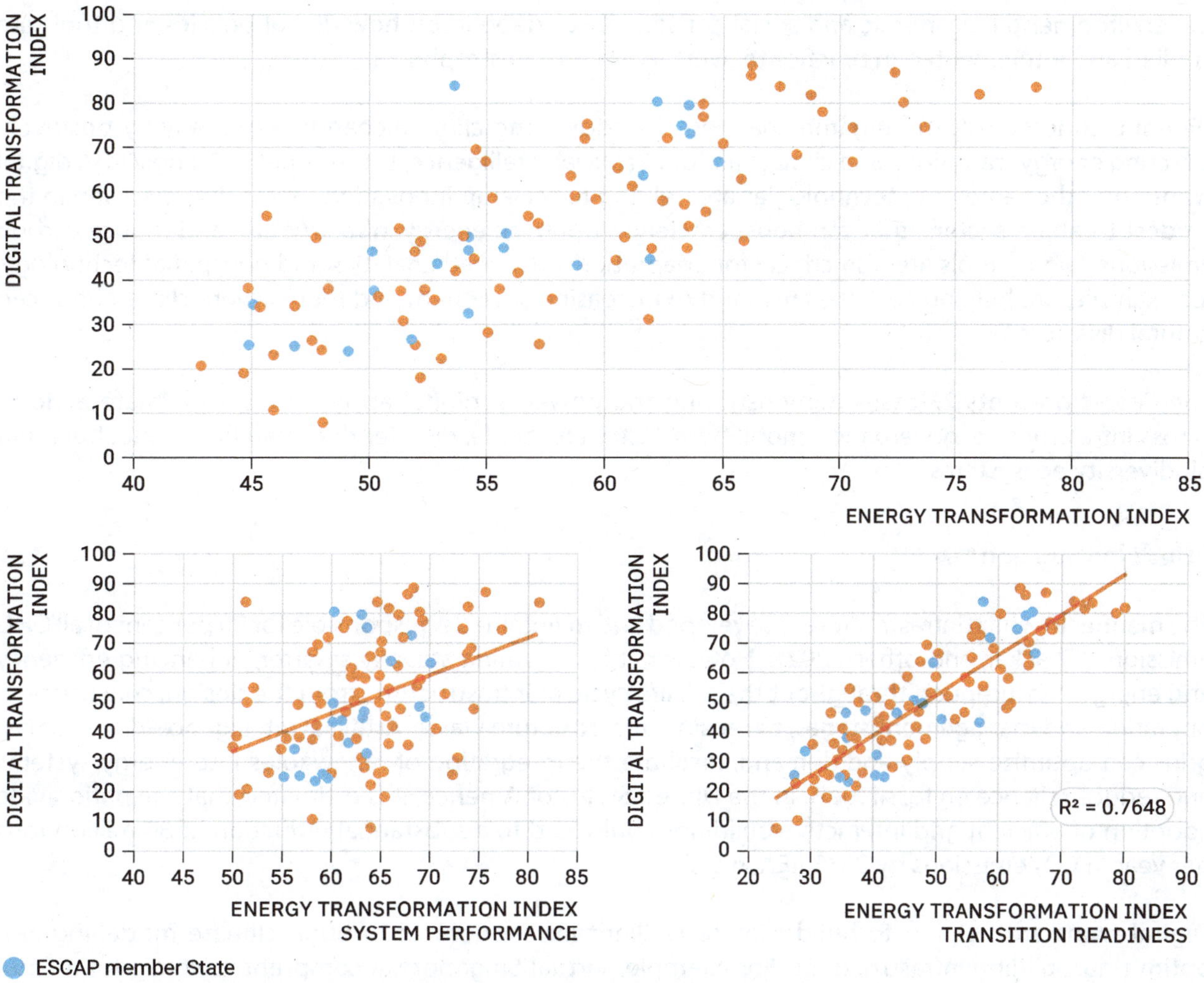

Source: Analysed by ESCAP, using data from the World Economic Forum, "Energy Transition Index", 2024. Available at https://initiatives.weforum.org/energy-and-industry-transition-intelligence/energy-transition-index.

FIGURE V-B Energy Transition Index System Performance (ETI-SP) and Energy Transition Index Transition Readiness (ETI-TR) by Digital Transformation Index (DTI) Grades

Source: Analysed by ESCAP, using data from the World Economic Forum, "Energy Transition Index", 2024. Available at https://initiatives.weforum.org/energy-and-industry-transition-intelligence/energy-transition-index.

Digital applications for climate action

Digital transformations are helping to power countries to new levels of economic development, but the environmental, economic and social consequences depend on how digital policies and tools are applied and implemented in practice to avert a climate catastrophe.

Digital technologies can be game changers for addressing climate change, especially by positively affecting energy transitions and climate action. Artificial intelligence, the Internet of Things (IoT), digital twins and other emerging technologies are helping to scale up innovations and solutions, even in the hardest-to-abate sectors, that can boost efficiency, optimize energy infrastructure and reduce carbon emissions. Digital tools are also critical for adaptation: advanced analytics and geospatial technology, for example, are helping countries respond to increasingly frequent and more severe climate-induced natural disasters.

The *Report* presents 27 cases demonstrating the power of digital applications for climate actions, across infrastructure, governance, mobility, industry and trade, disaster risk reduction, agriculture and biodiversity ecosystems.

Smart infrastructure

The manner in which infrastructure is developed and maintained is responsible for 79 per cent of all GHG emissions (Thacker, and others, 2021). However, it is becoming steadily smarter, enhancing efficiency and energy consumption throughout the full life cycle of infrastructure, from the design, construction, operation and management stages, to reusing infrastructure waste. Artificial intelligence-driven smart grids can optimize supply and demand, facilitate the integration of renewables into energy systems and reduce reliance on fossil fuels. In the United States of America, it is estimated that the nationwide adoption of efficient grid interactive buildings could lead to a substantial reduction of 80 million tons per year in CO_2 emissions by 2030 (IEA, n.d.a).

Digital twins are helping to build climate-resilient infrastructures through climate modelling and optimizing building infrastructures. For example, Virtual Singapore, a comprehensive digital twin of the city-state, can be used to assess and predict the impact of climate change on infrastructure, and enhance disaster preparedness by allowing simulations to guide the development of pre-emptive actions.

Digital technologies can cut emissions from landfill sites by making waste management smarter, creating circular processes, and improving rates of recycling. In the Republic of Korea, sensors combined with AI are helping to reduce toxic emissions from incinerators (APN News, 2021), while radio-frequency identification-based systems are being used to reduce and recycle food waste (Murdie, and Borsi, 2023).

Digital government

Governments across Asia and the Pacific are using digital tools and platforms to enhance public services, access to information and citizen participation, including increasing adaptive capacity and resilience of society by providing early warnings through mobile applications. Digital identification (ID) systems contribute to the reduction of material use, for example, by eliminating paper- and plastic-based IDs and the need to travel to government offices or to commercial services, such as banks. With digital IDs, there are numerous benefits for strengthening climate adaptive capacity. For example, citizens affected by disaster events or who require humanitarian support can connect more easily with rescue teams and relief agencies to get the necessary services through digital identification and verification.

Smart transport

In Asia and the Pacific, transport demand and CO_2 emissions could increase by more than 50 per cent by 2050 (ESCAP, 2023c). Innovations for transforming transport include not just electric vehicles but also ride-sharing schemes and public transport systems that take full advantage of satellite navigation, AI, Internet of Things (IoT) wireless networks, big data and 5G telecommunications networks (ESCAP, 2023b). Some cities in Asia and the Pacific have integrated ticketing systems that provide 'mobility as a service',[3] such as Beijing, China, which introduced the 'Mobility for Green City' initiative, which includes a carbon credit-inclusive incentive scheme to encourage participation (Mobility Transition in China, 2021).

While the transition to electric vehicles is underway, it is also important to improve the fuel efficiency of all vehicles, such as through the use of digital platforms to optimize logistic systems. In Greater Dhaka, Bangladesh, the digitalization of bus operations and management through a real-time bus management and information system is estimated to avoid up to 63,000 tons of carbon emissions on an annual basis.[4]

Smart industry

In the Asia-Pacific region, the industrial sector accounts for an estimated 24.5 per cent of carbon emissions by sector (IEA, n.d.b). Many companies are investing in cleaner and more efficient technologies, including using renewable energy sources like solar and wind power, and integrating smart solutions to promote sustainable industries. In Indonesia, with the third largest aquaculture industry globally, e-Fishery developed IoT mobile-based smart feeders which are boosting the productivity and efficiency of more than 200,000 aquaculture farmers (eFishery, 2023).

Digital trade facilitation

Digitalization is enabling climate-smart digital trade, helping to reduce trade costs and make global supply chains more resilient. For example, the Framework Agreement on Facilitation of Cross-Border Paperless Trade in Asia and the Pacific envisages automated customs and paperless trade agreements that process information digitally, which could save an estimated 13 million tons of CO_2 annually.

Digital data centres

Data centres constitute the core of the digital society and economy, powering everything from online commerce, to AI, to all manner of government services. By 2026, global electricity consumption of data centres, cryptocurrencies and AI is expected to range between 620–1050 TWh (IEA, 2024). However, energy consumption can be reduced by more sophisticated energy management systems, particularly for cooling, and using AI to constantly adjust operations. Measures to boost the sustainability of data centres are also important. For example, at the United Nations Information Communication Technology Facility in Valencia, all power which covers the data centre's electricity consumption is provided by a solar farm comprising 3,800 solar panels and 69 inverters, which since 2012 have prevented the release of 1,334,163 kg of carbon emissions into the atmosphere (United Nations Global Service Centre, n.d.).

---

3 'Mobility as a service' is a type of service that enables users to plan, book and pay for multiple types of mobility services through an integrated platform.

4 For more information, see United Nations Environment Programme (UNEP), and United Nations Climate Technology Centre and Network (UNCTCN), "Development of framework for real-time transport information systems for public transport in Greater Dhaka", 20 September 2020. Available at https://www.ctc-n.org/technical-assistance/projects/development-framework-real-time-transport-information-systems-public

Disaster risk reduction

Digital technologies are helping to reduce the risks and improve disaster management, cutting both human casualties and economic losses. Accurate and timely information on climate risks is now available from space technology applications involving satellite-generated data and geographic information systems, combined with generative AI applications and big data analytics. In East and North-East Asia, for example, the steep fall in mortality and economic losses from typhoons can be attributed to impact-based forecasting and risk-informed early warning products (ESCAP, 2019). ESCAP's SatGPT developed in partnership with the United Nations University Institute for Water, Environment and Health, leverages Large Language Models and cloud computing platforms to plot the flood hotspots.[5] The Starlink constellation of satellites has provided emergency communication services using satellites, such as after the twin tropical cyclones Judy and Kevin in Vanuatu in 2023, and the eruption of the Hunga Tonga-Hunga Ha'apai volcano in Tonga in 2022.

Agriculture and biodiversity ecosystems

Higher temperatures, irregular rainfall and extended periods of drought are creating harsher conditions for agriculture and biodiversity ecosystems. Smallholder farmers, who are disproportionately affected, can benefit from digital solutions that address climate shocks and stressors. In Pakistan, BaKhabar Kissan is a digital platform providing farmers with weather information and agricultural expertise.[6] In Nepal, the digital platform Aloi is helping smallholder dairy farmers to access loans for investing in agricultural inputs when coping with lower crops of livestock forage.[7] Digital solutions are also helping to improve the efficiency of natural resource management and address biodiversity loss. In Thailand, the Monsoon Tea Company is developing a mobile biodiversity traceability app which makes tea products traceable from end-to-end, and collects data on biodiversity using AI-powered biosensors.[8]

Envisioning future scenarios

The interaction of digital transformations with climate change can result in multiple, complex outcomes. The *Report* sets out three possible scenarios: positive, negative, or neutral, to inform the ways of steering transformations toward the most productive paths.

The positive scenario

In this scenario, digital transformations reduce long-term carbon emissions by enhancing energy efficiency and accelerating innovation solutions and climate technologies for mitigation and adaptation. Well-designed policies, regulatory frameworks and sustained investments in digital technologies, data and integrated digital platforms support climate action. The positive scenario can result from three main effects:

The efficiency effect – Digital transformation improves efficiency and optimizes existing infrastructure, as well as boosts supply and demand across sectors. According to the International Energy Association, the deployment of digital technologies and big data could save $80 billion per year or around 5 per cent of total world annual power generation costs, while digitalization can help the integration of renewables by enabling smart grids to better match energy demand (IEA, 2017).

---

5 SatGPT can be accessed at https://satgpt.net/

6 For more information on BaKhabar Kissan (BKK), see https://www.gsma.com/solutions-and-impact/connectivity-for-good/mobile-for-development/digital-grantees-portfolio/bakhabar-kissan-bkk/

7 For more information on Aloi, see https://www.gsma.com/solutions-and-impact/connectivity-for-good/mobile-for-development/digital-grantees-portfolio/aloi/

8 For more information on the Monsoon Tea Company, see https://www.gsma.com/solutions-and-impact/connectivity-for-good/mobile-for-development/digital-grantees-portfolio/monsoon-tea-company/

The substitution effect – Digital technologies help to replace physical needs and processes with digital and virtual alternatives, contributing to both dematerialization and decarbonization that help shrink carbon footprints. For example, the virtualization of business processes and move toward remote working have transformed the ways in which individuals, companies and governments operate and communicate. In April 2020, compared to peak-2019 levels, during the COVID-19 lockdowns, dramatic changes in mobility, production and consumption patterns temporarily reduced global carbon emissions by 17 per cent (Le Quéré, and others, 2020).

The combinatorial effect – Ever-changing interactions and synergies between foundational and emerging technologies, particularly the rise of AI, are accelerating the advance of energy-saving and emissions-reduction technologies. These present tremendous opportunities to accelerate the transition towards low-carbon infrastructure and renewable energy sources, and advance toward efficient, interconnected energy systems and net-zero carbon emissions.

The negative scenario

In this scenario, as countries move toward digital economies, soaring energy demands from digitally-driven devices and services outweigh productivity gains. The digital economy confronts the dual challenge of meeting the increasing energy demands of inclusive digital societies and addressing the mounting climate concerns. The negative scenario can result from three main factors:

Proliferation of digital devices and data centres with the demands of AI – With the expansion of digital infrastructure, including data centres and more intensive use of AI, total carbon emissions increase across product life cycles; from production to distribution to consumption to disposal.

Uneven investment in climate technologies – Another issue is the uneven capital investments in climate technologies due to market conditions. Insufficient carbon-mitigating private capital investment goes into sectors that generate the biggest shares of global emissions, as the expectation is that the capital investments into these sectors will come from governments and other providers.

End-user demand increases carbon footprints – Consumer preferences, choices and behaviour are being reshaped by digital connectivity and IoT. Smartphones, smart home applications and social media are changing the way people work and relate to each other, with important implications for business models and the overall industry landscape.

The neutral scenario

In this case, the net impact of digital transformation on climate change is neither positive nor negative. Despite the positive contribution of digital technologies to climate action, the increasing energy use and the resulting carbon emissions from the digital economy roughly offset the benefits of digital transformation for climate action, so the result is broadly neutral.

Whether digital transformations help or hinder climate action has been a subject of scientific debate. But the extent to which digital transformation contributes to climate change will clearly depend on a country's technological capacity, industrial structure and deliberate policy and regulatory measures.

Digital destinations: policy recommendations

Across Asia and the Pacific, countries differ widely in their levels of technological capacity, regulatory policies, industry structures, existing infrastructure, digital culture and behaviour patterns. The region faces several barriers to the adoption of digital solutions, including the lack of adequate digital infrastructure, particularly in rural and remote areas, the gender digital divide in the use of Internet and mobile devices, disparities in digital and technological skills across demographics, as well as the costs and challenges of accessing sophisticated technologies between digitally advanced and developing countries.

Each country has its own specific features of the digital-growth-climate nexus and can adopt policies tailored to its specific context, but there are common elements, such as the need for policies to be inclusive, as those most vulnerable to the impacts of climate change could be those most disproportionately affected by the digital divide, while the rise of new technologies and automation also has potentially adverse implications for workers if not accompanied by digital upskilling.

Digitally advanced countries, for example, could prioritize climate mitigation and adaptation particularly, in the services sector, and sharing green technologies for climate action with developing countries. Other countries that are digitally progressing can focus on enhancing energy efficiency and transitions in manufacturing and industrial sectors. Countries that are digitally lagging, may focus first on agriculture and green investments in digital infrastructure and connectivity, along with measures for bridging digital divides.

Building on the five pillars of ESCAP's Digital Transformation Framework, the *Report* makes the following recommendations:

 ### Pillar 1: Infrastructure and network

Invest in resilient digital infrastructure and network systems, in particular, efficient renewable energy infrastructure and modular infrastructure systems that take advantage of co-deployment of fibre-optic cables along linear infrastructures such as power grids, highways and railways. Deploying such integrated infrastructure solutions is not only cost-effective, but also key for communication systems that underlie smart infrastructure. Relatedly, pursuing open-source applications, and opportunities for sharing software and design can lead to finding collective knowledge-based solutions and scaling up the impact of digital solutions on climate mitigation and adaptation efforts.

 ### Pillar 2: Government

Integrate digital technologies for climate action across ministries and national policy and planning processes, while strengthening stakeholders' engagement. Towards this end, it is recommended that software applications and big data, to the extent possible given varying national contexts, be kept in the public open domain, while policy officials need to be enabled to continuously acquire the skills and knowledge necessary to harness the benefits and minimize the risks of emerging technologies.

 ### Pillar 3: Business

Boost investments in low-carbon markets, green and climate technologies, and renewable energy infrastructures by filling the gaps between short-term investment and long-term returns. Enhance business sustainability by adopting lower carbon production and consumption processes and leveraging digital technologies to optimize efficiency. Such actions should go in line with promoting sustainability across business strategies and actions, including integrating environmental, social and governance metrics to help reduce adverse environmental and social impacts, and committing to net-zero in business operations with clear and credible timelines.

 Pillar 4: People

Raise public awareness and support for the effective use of digital products and services, as well as share information on the risks and challenges in adopting rapid digital transformation and their impact on society and in particular, vulnerable populations. This needs to be complemented by investment in lifelong digital skills so that behavioural changes in the sustainable use of new technologies are driven by whole-of-society bottom-up approaches.

 Pillar 5: Ecosystem

Governments and businesses can work together through public-private partnerships, where researchers, policymakers and businesses can build knowledge and cooperative networks to share the latest research findings and solutions. More extensive availability of open-access data, taking into account national contexts, as well as data interoperability are essential in facilitating the use of data, while the development of tools to measure the impacts of digital transformation actions on the Sustainable Development Goals at the target and indicator levels remains important.

The Asia-Pacific region has an unparalleled digital transformation opportunity to pursue sustainable and inclusive economic growth and mitigate climate risks in a positive-sum game, to accelerate the implementation of the Sustainable Development Goals. With the transboundary nature of economic, social and environmental challenges that is beyond the ability of any single country to address, regional cooperation is imperative for governments across Asia and the Pacific to build an inclusive digital future, extend connectivity to all, and harness new technologies to confront the challenges of climate change and environmental degradation.

In this regard, members and associate member States of ESCAP can strengthen cooperative actions and their implementation through the Asia-Pacific Information Superhighway Initiative and its Action Plan 2022–2026, adopted as resolution 79/10 in May 2023. In addition, through Resolution 80/1 in April 2024, in which ESCAP members and associate members welcomed the convening of the Asia-Pacific Ministerial Conference on Digital Inclusion and Transformation in September 2024 in Kazakhstan, it is expected that Ministers will embark on a visionary and ambitious blueprint for regional digital cooperation, that accelerates implementation of the Asia-Pacific Information Superhighway Initiative and its Action Plan 2022–2026 in support of the Sustainable Development Goals (SDGs) and other regional technology initiatives.

Only in a spirit of collaboration can countries in Asia and the Pacific leverage the opportunities presented by digital innovations to bring about transformative change that will support national and regional efforts to avert a climate catastrophe.

Executive Summary References

APN News (2021). SK ecoplant Develops eco-friendly AI-powered incinerator solution using AWS. 13 July. Available at https://www.apnnews.com/sk-ecoplant-develops-eco-friendly-ai-powered-incinerator-solution-using-aws/

eFishery (2023). Growing together with more than 200,000 farmers across 280 cities in Indonesia. Available at https://efishery.com/en/

Global Carbon Budget Data Hub (2023). Available at https://globalcarbonbudget.org/carbonbudget2023/

International Energy Agency (IEA) (2017). *Digitalisation and Energy*. Paris. Available at https://www.iea.org/reports/digitalisation-and-energy

__________ (2024). *Electricity 2024*. Paris. Available at https://www.iea.org/reports/electricity-2024

__________ (n.d.a). *Efficient Grid-Interactive Buildings: Future of buildings in ASEAN*. Available at https://iea.blob.core.windows.net/assets/71d1b69d-e8aa-49e5-9e0c-12c13d5a3a1f/EfficientGrid-InteractiveBuildings.pdf

__________ (n.d.b). Total CO_2 emissions. Available at https://www.iea.org/regions/asia-pacific/emissions

Le Quéré, Corinne, and others (2020). Temporary reduction in daily global CO_2 emissions during the COVID-19 forced confinement. *Nature Climate Change*, vol. 10 (May). Available at https://www.nature.com/articles/s41558-020-0797-x

Mobility Transition in China (2021). Beijing MaaS Platform Launches "MaaS Mobility for Green City" Initiative. 26 May. Available at https://transition-china.org/mobilityposts/beijing-maas-platform-launches-maas-mobility-for-green-city-initiative/

Murdie, Meghan, and Aurore Borsi (2023). Solving the food waste disposal issue in South Korea. Circle Economy Foundation – Knowledge Hub. 23 March. Available at https://knowledge-hub.circle-economy.com/article/22916

Our World in Data (n.d.). Share of global CO_2 emissions. Available at https://ourworldindata.org/grapher/annual-share-of-co2-emissions

Thacker, S., and others (2021). Infrastructure for Climate Action. United Nations Office for Project Services (UNOPS). Copenhagen, Denmark. Available at https://www.unep.org/resources/report/infrastructure-climate-action

United Nations Economic and Social Commission for Asia and the Pacific (ESCAP) (2019). *Asia-Pacific Disaster Report 2019: The Disaster Riskscape across Asia-Pacific: Pathways for Resilience, Inclusion and Empowerment*. United Nations publication.

__________ (2022a). *Asia-Pacific Digital Transformation Report 2022: Shaping our Digital Future*. United Nations publication.

__________ (2022b). New UN report reveals that climate pledges by countries in the Asia-Pacific are off track with the 1.5°C pathway. Bangkok. 4 November. Available at https://www.unescap.org/news/new-un-report-reveals-climate-pledges-countries-asia-pacific-are-track-15degc-pathway

__________ (2023a). *Asia-Pacific Disaster Report 2023: Seizing the Moment: Targeting Transformative Disaster Risk Resilience*. United Nations publication.

__________ (2023b). Regional Road Map to Support Regional Cooperation for the Wider Deployment of Sustainable Smart Transport Systems in Asia and the Pacific. Bangkok, Thailand.

__________ (2023c). *The Race to Net Zero: Accelerating Climate Action in Asia and the Pacific*. United Nations publication.

United Nations Economic and Social Commission for Asia and the Pacific (ESCAP), and others (2023). *2023 Review of Climate Ambition in Asia and the Pacific: Just Transition towards Regional Net-zero Climate Resilient Development*. United Nations publication.

United Nations Global Service Centre (n.d.). Available at https://www.ungsc.org/

Digital big bang in a climate crisis

Climate change and digital transformations may appear distinct phenomena, but the two forces are intricately interlinked and remarkably transforming our society and economy. In Asia and the Pacific, as in the rest of the world, the climate crisis and technological advances intersect and interconnect through a complex mix of hazards and opportunities, creating a series of vicious, but also potentially virtuous cycles.

Currently, the defining global challenge is climate change. Asia and the Pacific, in particular, is home to six of the top ten global carbon emitters and contributes more than half of the world's total greenhouse gases (GHGs). At the same time, the region is highly vulnerable to the consequences of climate catastrophes, notably through more frequent extreme weather events and other disasters that hit the poorest people hardest and cause widespread destruction. In addition to human causalities, average annual economic losses increased from $924 billion to almost $1 trillion (ESCAP, 2023).

FIGURE 1-1 Global CO_2 emissions trend, 1900–2023

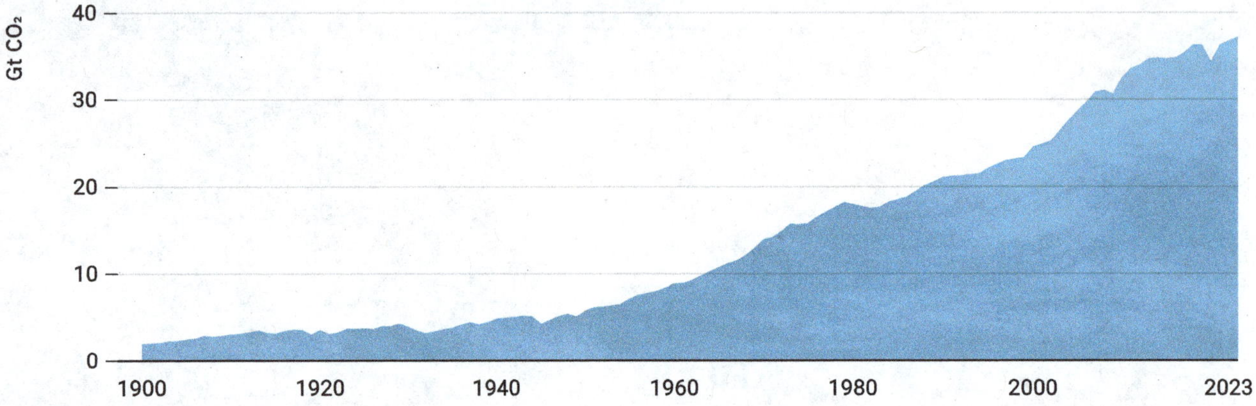

Source: International Energy Agency (IEA), "CO_2 Emissions in 2023" (Paris, 2024b). Available at https://www.iea.org/reports/co2-emissions-in-2023

Figure 1-1 tracks the increase in global emissions over the past century. While the trend is alarming and dangerous, it can be slowed and even reined in if policymakers act now. Many countries in Asia and the Pacific are determined to address the climate crisis and are raising their ambitions and increasing their commitments, through international forums, such as the United Nations Framework Convention on Climate Change (UNFCCC), the Intergovernmental Panel on Climate Change (IPCC), and the Conference of the Parties (COP). For example, in 2015, Asia-Pacific countries adopted the Paris Agreement and established nationally determined contributions (NDCs).

These commitments are being pursued within a constantly shifting technological landscape. In this *Report*, the term digital transformation goes beyond the digitalization of goods and services. It represents a new development paradigm, reweaving the whole fabric of society, in terms of value creation, management, use and distribution through applications of disruptive technologies, including AI, digital data, connectivity and networks (ESCAP, 2022, p. 16).

The ways in which countries do business, deliver public services, and protect people and the planet are continually being transformed, and often turbocharged, by digital innovations. The most recent public interactions have been through Chat GPT and other freely available AI bots. Less visible are pervasive connectivity and the flows of digital data surging through ever-expanding private and public networks.

These data flows are also reshaping the ways in which countries are governed. Global public policy and action as well as many public services are becoming "digital by default" (ESCAP, 2022, p. 34). Indeed, frontier technologies and big data are reshaping societies across Asia and the Pacific and will profoundly influence the 2030 Agenda for Sustainable Development, as well as the prospects of avoiding a climate catastrophe.

1.1 Digital demands for energy

The most immediate impact of any digital device is its consumption of energy. Between 2012 and 2022, the global stock of network-connected digital devices increased from 0.56 billion to 11 billion (IEA, 2023) (Figure 1-2). Switching on each of these absorbs yet more electrical power and expands the digital carbon footprint. By 2026, global electricity consumption of data centres, cryptocurrencies and AI is expected to range between 620–1050 TWh (IEA, 2024).

FIGURE 1-2 Global stock of network-connected digital devices, 2010–2022

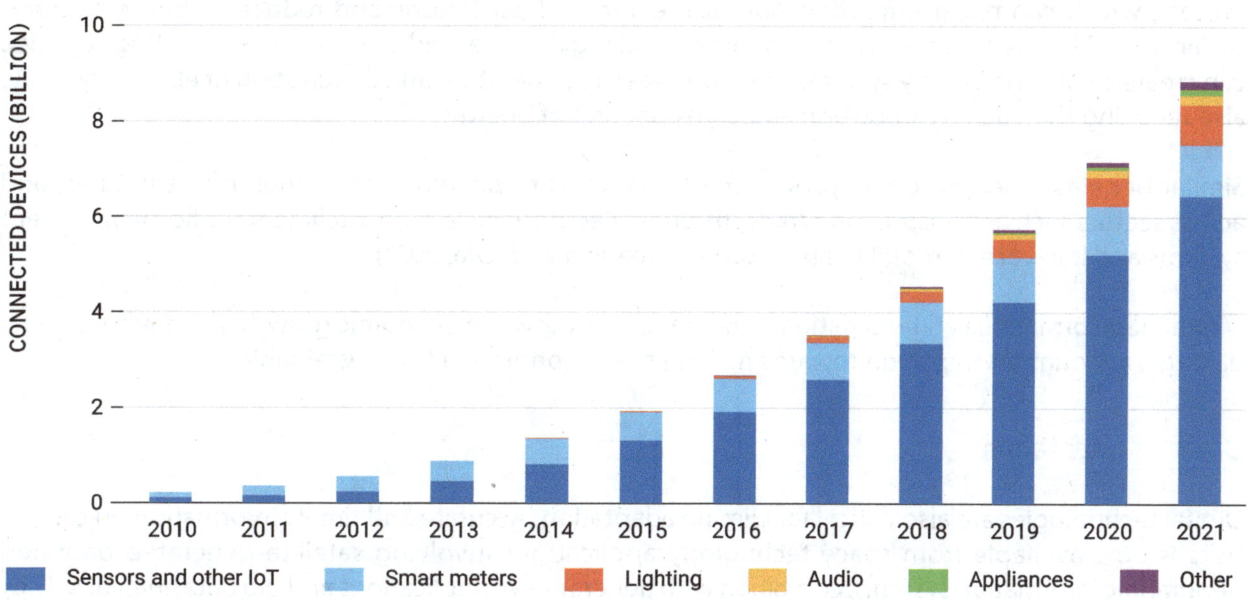

Source: International Energy Agency (IEA), "Global stock of digitally enabled automated devices, 2010–2021", 25 August 2022. Available at https://www.iea.org/data-and-statistics/charts/global-stock-of-digitally-enabled-automated-devices-2010-2021

As well as consuming energy directly, the mass digitalization that is smartening everything from tractors to toasters is also making new devices and activities more affordable. Between 1974 and 2019, global electricity consumption for industry, residential, and commercial and public services sectors nearly quadrupled (Figure 1-3).

FIGURE 1-3 World electricity final consumption by sector, 1974–2019

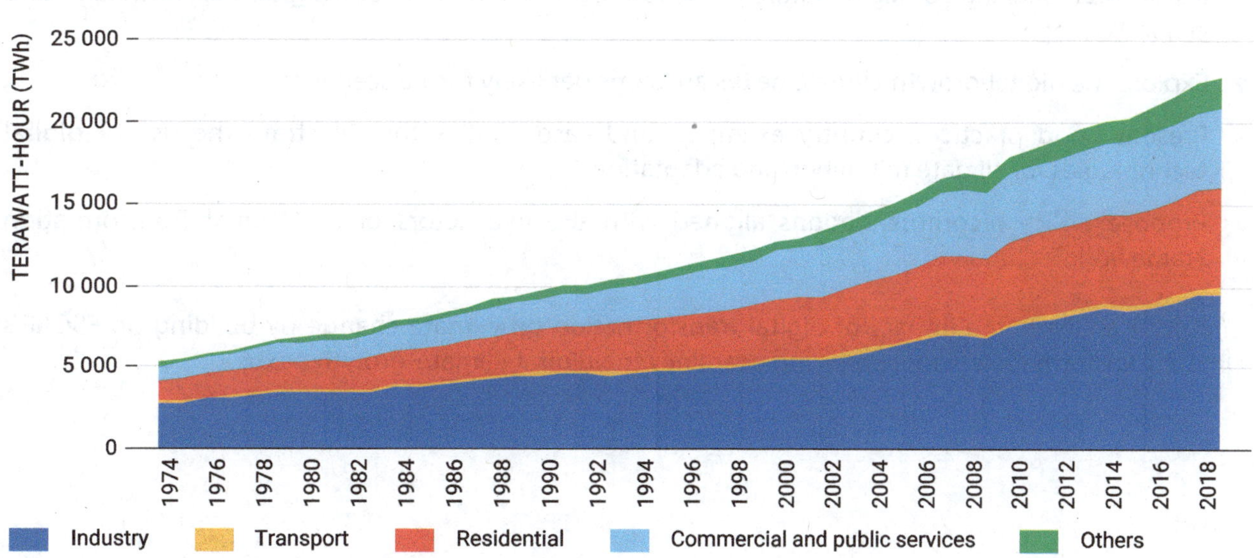

Source: International Energy Agency (IEA), "World electricity final consumption by sector, 1974–2019", 6 August 2021. Available at https://www.iea.org/data-and-statistics/charts/world-electricity-final-consumption-by-sector-1974-2019

1.2 Digital transformation for climate action

The more intensive use of digital devices is increasing world energy consumption, but the relationship between the two is complex, since digital transformations can also help reduce long-term energy consumption and serve as a catalyst for climate action.

Smarter energy optimization

Digital technologies are helping to scale up innovations and solutions, even in the hardest-to-abate sectors, which can boost efficiency, optimize energy infrastructure, and reduce carbon emissions. Artificial intelligence using analytics, algorithms and big data, backed by powerful computing capacity, can create smart grid energy systems that optimize the generation and distribution of electricity, while also reducing the quantity of carbon emissions per unit of energy.

Similar benefits emerge from applying smarter systems to buildings and other infrastructures, and across sectors such as transport and trade, through electric vehicles and intelligent traffic management systems and low-carbon mobility and logistics (Aparicio and 'Ofa, 2021).

Digital transformation can help mitigate the trade-offs between economic growth and environmental damage, as countries transition towards making their economies more sustainable.

Smarter adaptation

Digital technologies are also critical for climate adaptation. Accurate and timely information on climate risks is now available from space technology applications involving satellite-generated data and geographic information systems, combined with generative AI applications and big data analytics. They are being used to measure rainfall patterns, forest cover, water quality, and impacts on biodiversity, and can also enable more accurate weather forecasts that feed into disaster early warning systems. At the same time, digital technologies are making devices and processes for agriculture and infrastructure smarter, more efficient and climate resilient.

This *Report* considers how digital transformations will structurally impact the trajectory of climate change. Specifically, it will:

1   Use the Digital Transformation Framework first introduced in the *Asia-Pacific Digital Transformation Report 2022: Shaping our digital future* to explore connections between digital transformation and climate change.

2   Explore the digital-growth-climate nexus and consider likely future scenarios.

3   Present good practices, country examples and case studies that illustrate the use of digital technologies for climate mitigation and adaptation.

4   Propose policy recommendations aligned with the five actors of the Digital Transformation Framework.[9]

Chapter 2 analyses the impact of digital transformation on climate change by building on ESCAP's Digital Transformation Framework, and examines the digital-climate-growth nexus.

---

9   By using the five pillars: infrastructure and network, government, business, people, and ecosystem.

Chapter 3 showcases good practices and country examples of digital applications in addressing climate change, in terms of mitigation and adaptation. These can involve the use of AI, IoT, big data, digital twins, geospatial technologies and others, which have been employed in infrastructure, government, mobility, industry and trade, digital data centres, disaster risk reduction, agriculture and biodiversity ecosystems.

Chapter 4 explores key drivers of digital transformation for climate change and outlines three future scenarios.

Chapter 5 summarizes the key findings of the *Report* and proposes policy actions aligned with the five actors of the Digital Transformation Index Framework.

Chapter 1 References

Aparicio, C. B., and S.V. 'Ofa (2021). Digital technologies for climate change adaptation in Asia and the Pacific. United Nations Economic and Social Commission for Asia and the Pacific (ESCAP), Information and Communications Technology and Disaster Risk Reduction Division. Working Paper Series. December. Bangkok. Available at https://www.unescap.org/sites/default/d8files/knowledge-products/Digital%20technologies%20for%20climate%20change%20adaptation%20in%20Asia%20and%20the%20Pacific.pdf

International Energy Agency (IEA) (2021). World electricity final consumption by sector, 1974–2019. 6 August. Available at https://www.iea.org/data-and-statistics/charts/world-electricity-final-consumption-by-sector-1974-2019

__________ (2022). Global stock of digitally enabled automated devices, 2010–2021. 25 August. Available at https://www.iea.org/data-and-statistics/charts/global-stock-of-digitally-enabled-automated-devices-2010-2021

__________ (2023). Global stock of digitally enabled automated devices, 2010–2021. 11 July. Available at https://www.iea.org/data-and-statistics/charts/global-stock-of-digitally-enabled-automated-devices-2010-2021-2

__________ (2024). *Electricity 2024*. Paris. Available at https://www.iea.org/reports/electricity-2024

United Nations Economic and Social Commission for Asia and the Pacific (ESCAP) (2022). *Asia-Pacific Digital Transformation Report 2022: Shaping our Digital Future*. United Nations publication.

__________ (2023). *Asia-Pacific Disaster Report 2023: Seizing the Moment: Targeting Transformative Disaster Risk Resilience*. United Nations publication.

The digital-growth-climate nexus

This chapter builds on ESCAP's Digital Transformation Framework to examine the relationships between digital transformations and climate change. It considers the correlations between digital transformations and economic growth, then adds a climate-change dimension to arrive at the digital-growth-climate nexus.

Data for this nexus indicates that emissions rise during the earlier periods of economic growth, but then start to fall as technological advancements become more sophisticated and efficient. A similar series of transitions occur with energy, underlining the importance of digital tools in the move toward greener energy systems.

2.1 Building on the Digital Transformation Framework

For tracking the progress of digital transformation, the *2022 Asia-Pacific Digital Transformation Report: Shaping Our Digital Future* introduced the Digital Transformation Index (DTI) Framework. This considered five actors of operation: network/infrastructure, government, business, people, and ecosystems, and measured their contribution at three stages of digital transformation; foundation, adoption and acceleration. In total, the DTI uses 105 indicators across the 15 separate domains (Figure 2-1).

FIGURE 2-1 The Digital Transformation Index (DTI) Framework

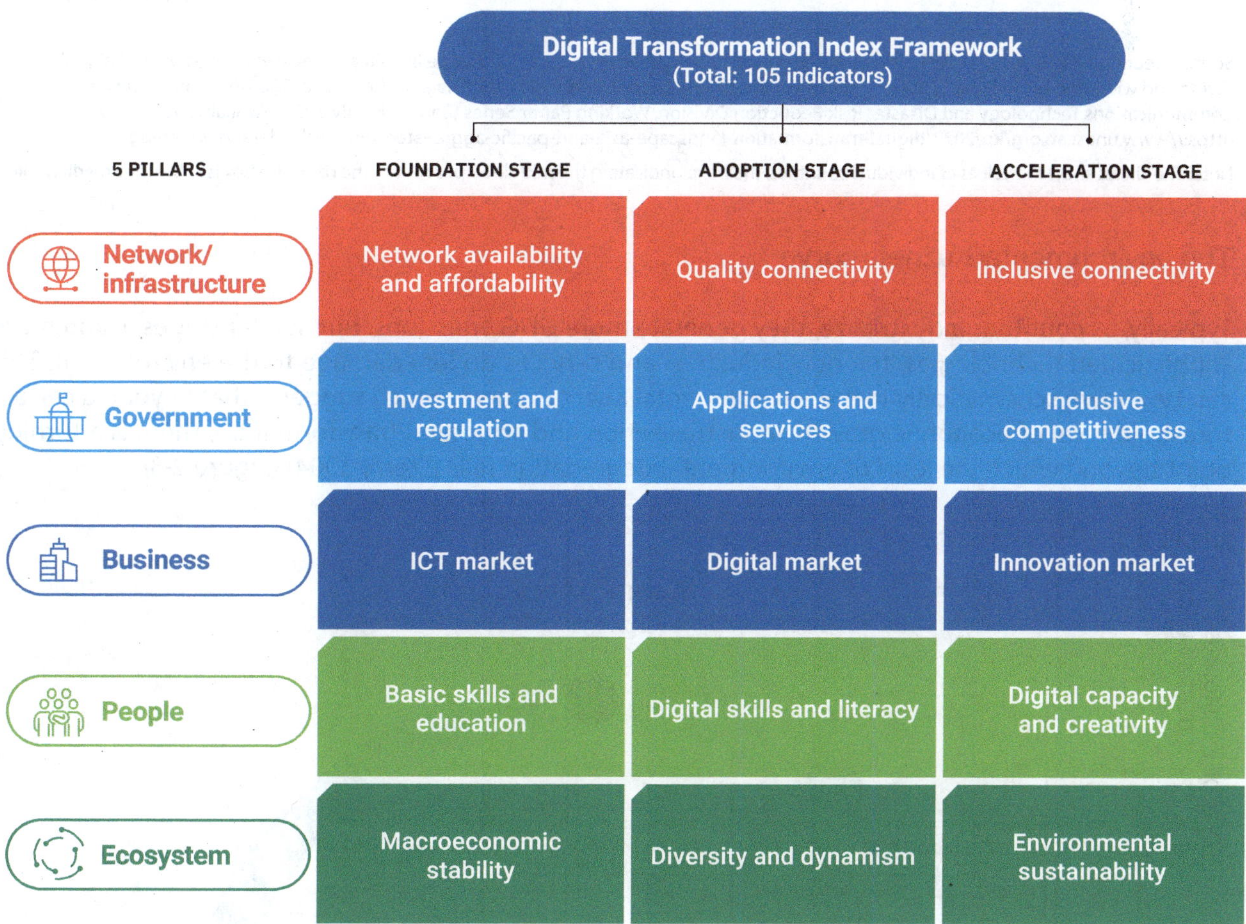

The *2022 Report* calculated the DTI of 107 countries and found that a country's digital capacity correlates strongly with its per capita GDP (Jun, Park, and Kim, 2022). This is illustrated in Figure 2-2. Generally, the higher-income countries have the higher digital transformation capacities, though some countries have achieved even more than their incomes might have indicated.

FIGURE 2-2 Digital Transformation Index (DTI) score distribution and average score by income level

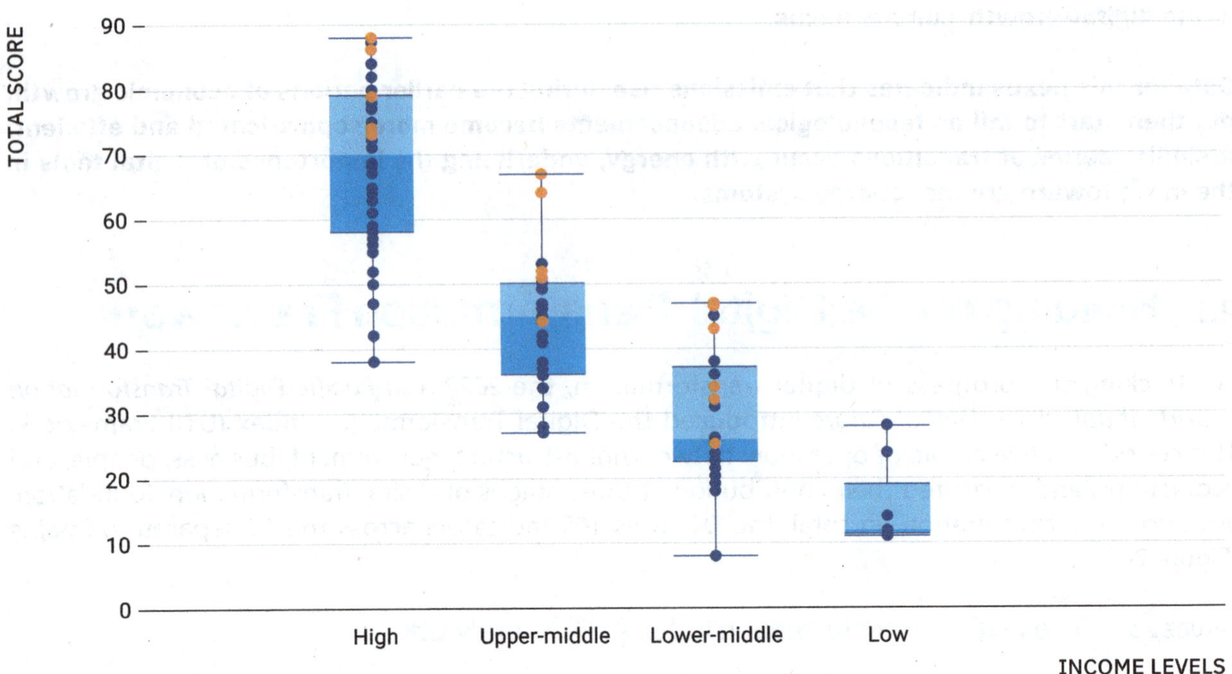

Source: Seunghwa Jun, Jongsur Park, and Jeong Yoon Kim, "Digital transformation landscape in Asia and the Pacific: Aggravated digital divide and widening growth gap", United Nations Economic and Social Commission for Asia and the Pacific (ESCAP), Information and Communications Technology and Disaster Risk Reduction Division, Working Paper Series (Bangkok, July 2022). Available at https://www.unescap.org/kp/2022/digital-transformation-landscape-asia-and-pacific-aggravated-digital-divide-and-widening

Note: The circles show the values of individual countries, the boxes indicating the middle 50 per cent of the data. The box is split at the median value.

The environmental Kuznets curve

Typically, as countries industrialize, they generate more GHG emissions, but at later stages, using more sophisticated technologies, the new industries and services do less damage to the environment. This can be shown schematically in the environmental Kuznets curve, which suggests that beyond a certain threshold level of economic growth, industrialization and structural transformation, there is a turning point beyond which the level of environmental degradation falls (Stern, 2004) (Figure 2-3).

FIGURE 2-3 Environmental Kuznets curve

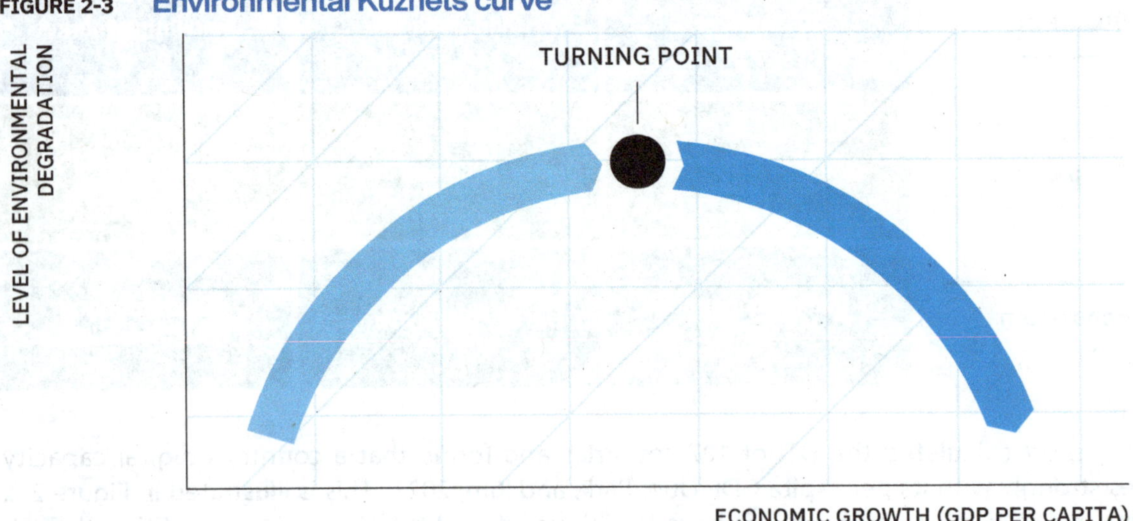

Source: ESCAP.

The digital-growth-climate nexus hypothesis

There is an equivalent pattern for carbon emissions. Historically, as per capita GDP rose in the more advanced countries, their CO_2 emissions rose in tandem. But, in later years their emissions started to decrease. This is illustrated in Figure 2-4.

FIGURE 2-4 CO_2 emissions in advanced economies, 1973–2023

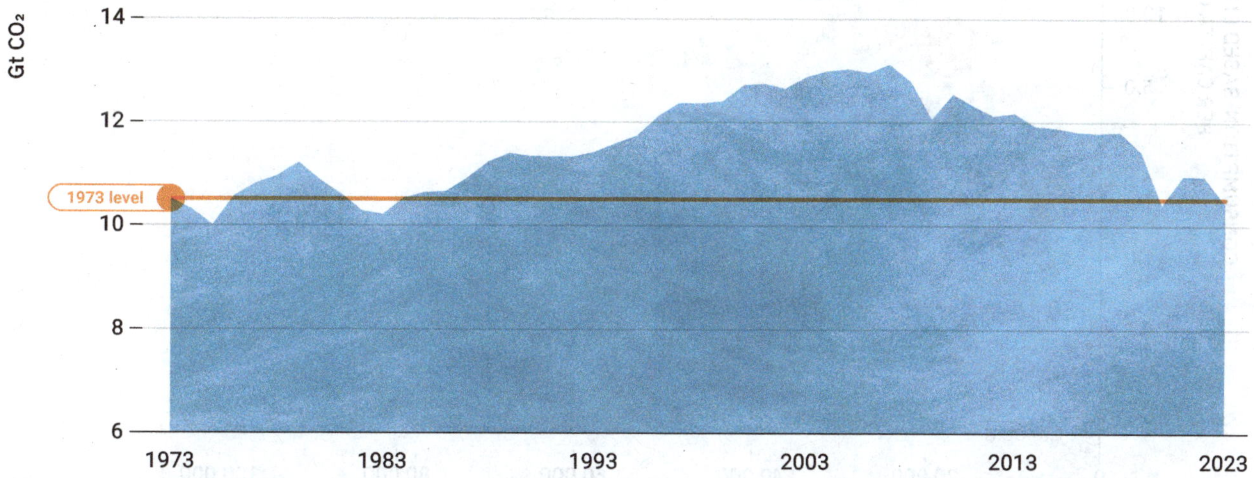

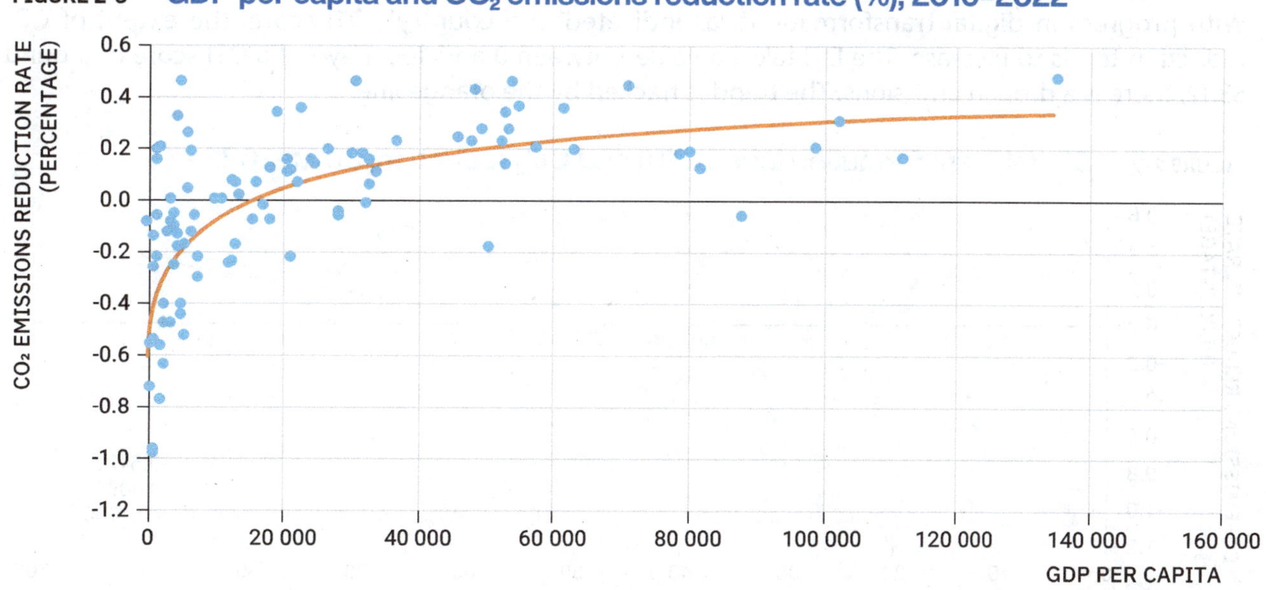

Source: International Energy Agency (IEA), "CO2 emissions from combustion in advanced economies, 1973–2023", 27 February 2024a. Available at https://www.iea.org/data-and-statistics/charts/co2-emissions-from-combustion-in-advanced-economies-1973-2023

By 2023, while the combined GDP of advanced counties increased by around 1.7 per cent in that year, their emissions had decreased to what they were 50 years earlier (IEA, 2024). This is illustrated in Figure 2-5 for a selection of countries,[10] for which emissions data are available from 2010 to 2022. Each dot represents a country placed according to its percentage drop in emissions between those two years and its per capita GDP (2022). The figure suggests that at lower levels of GDP, a number of countries saw an increase in emissions (a negative reduction), but countries at higher levels of GDP generally registered a decrease in their emissions. The switch starts at around $14,000–$20,000, after which the impacts start to level off by 20 to 40 per cent.

FIGURE 2-5   GDP per capita and CO_2 emissions reduction rate (%), 2010–2022

Source: Analysed by ESCAP. Data is from the Global Carbon Budget Data Hub, 2023. Available at https://globalcarbonbudget.org/carbonbudget2023/ and is processed by Our World in Data, "Share of global CO2 emissions", n.d. Available at https://ourworldindata.org/grapher/annual-share-of-co2-emissions

10 In total, 98 countries are included in the analysis, based on the availability of data.

As illustrated in Figure 2-6, a similar pattern emerges when considering consumption-based emissions per capita.

FIGURE 2-6 **Consumption-based CO$_2$ emissions per capita, and GDP per capita, 2021**

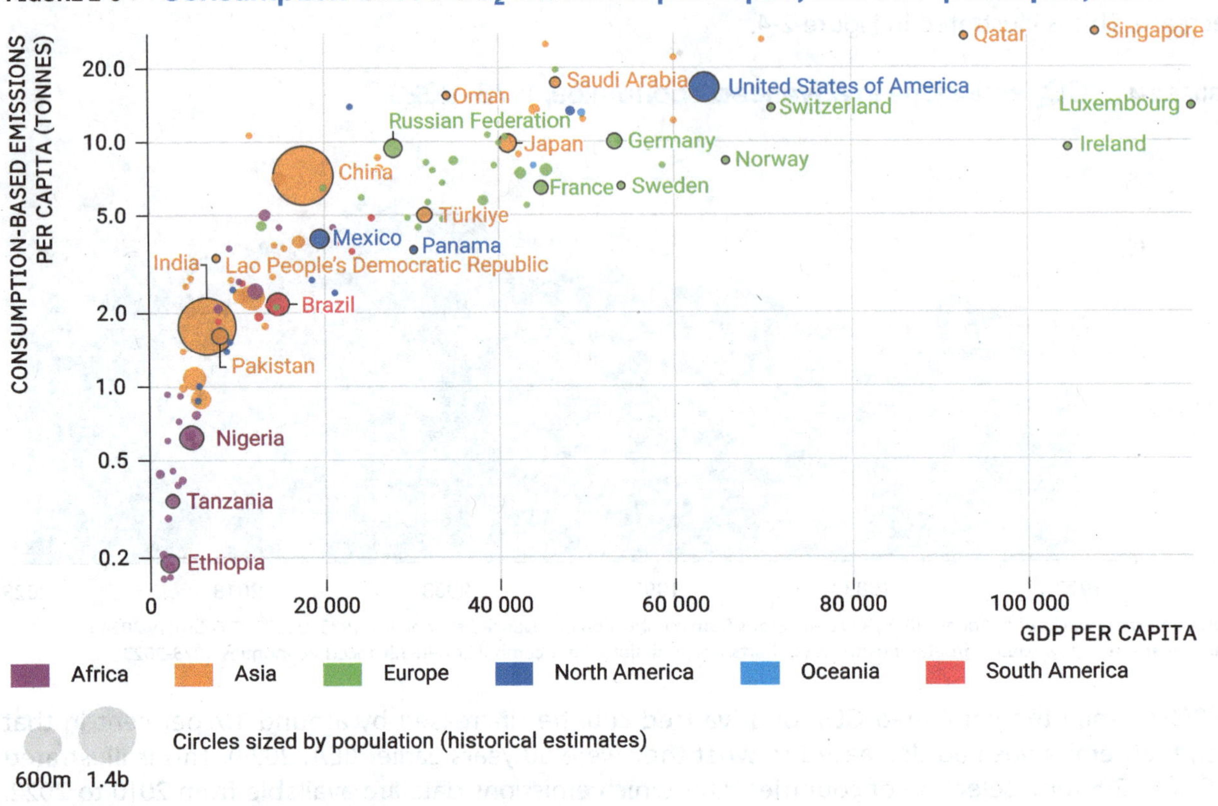

Source: Hannah Ritchie, Pablo Rosado and Max Roser, "CO2 and greenhouse gas emissions", Our World in Data, 2023.
Available at https://ourworldindata.org/co2-and-greenhouse-gas-emissions

These trends show emissions levelling off with overall economic output. But the reduction in emissions can also be correlated more precisely with advances in technology using the DTI. The results, indicating the values for individual countries, are presented in Figure 2-7.

With progress in digital transformations, as indicated in a country's DTI score, the extent of CO$_2$ reduction tends to increase. The DTI takes a value between 0 and 100. Beyond a DTI score of around 53.12, there is a drop in emissions. The trend is tracked by the orange line.

FIGURE 2-7 **Digital Transformation Index (DTI) and CO$_2$ reduction, 2010–2022**

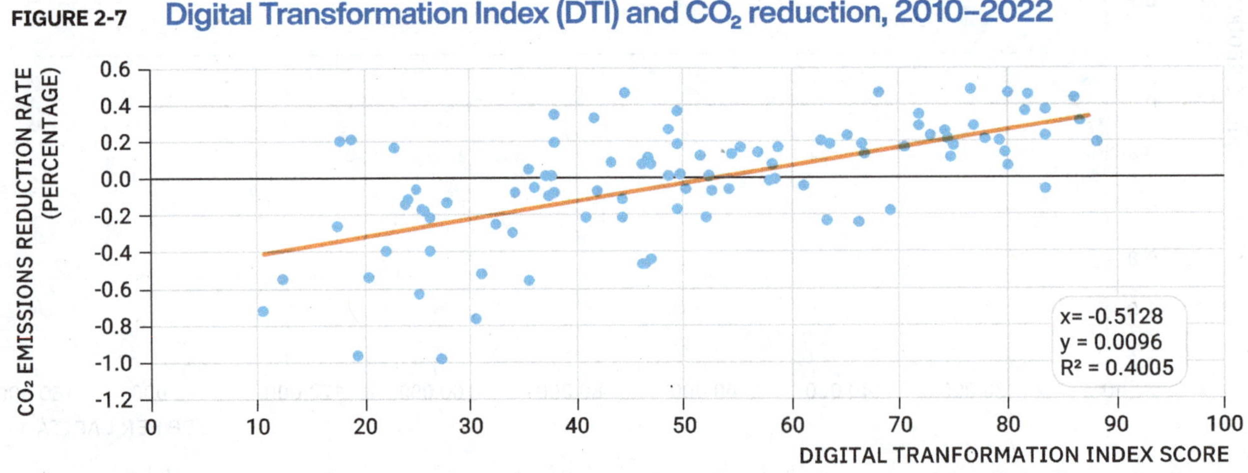

Source: Analysed by ESCAP. Data is from the Global Carbon Budget Data Hub, 2023. Available at https://globalcarbonbudget.org/carbonbudget2023/ and is processed by Our World in Data, "Share of global CO2 emissions", n.d. Available at https://ourworldindata.org/grapher/annual-share-of-co2-emissions

This analysis can also be applied to groups of countries. This is shown in Figure 2-8, which plots the percentage reduction by country income group using a box chart that displays both the median value for the group and the range. Over this period, high-income countries achieved a median 17 per cent drop in emissions, while the low-income countries saw an increase in emissions. In developing countries, economic growth is highly dependent on manufacturing processes that make intensive use of materials and are heavily dependent on fossil fuels. Such rapid urbanization and building of new infrastructure, increases the average energy consumption per unit of GDP, and the material footprints per capita, of these countries, are often higher than those in developed countries (IEA, 2021; UNEP, n.d.).

FIGURE 2-8　　CO_2 reduction by income group

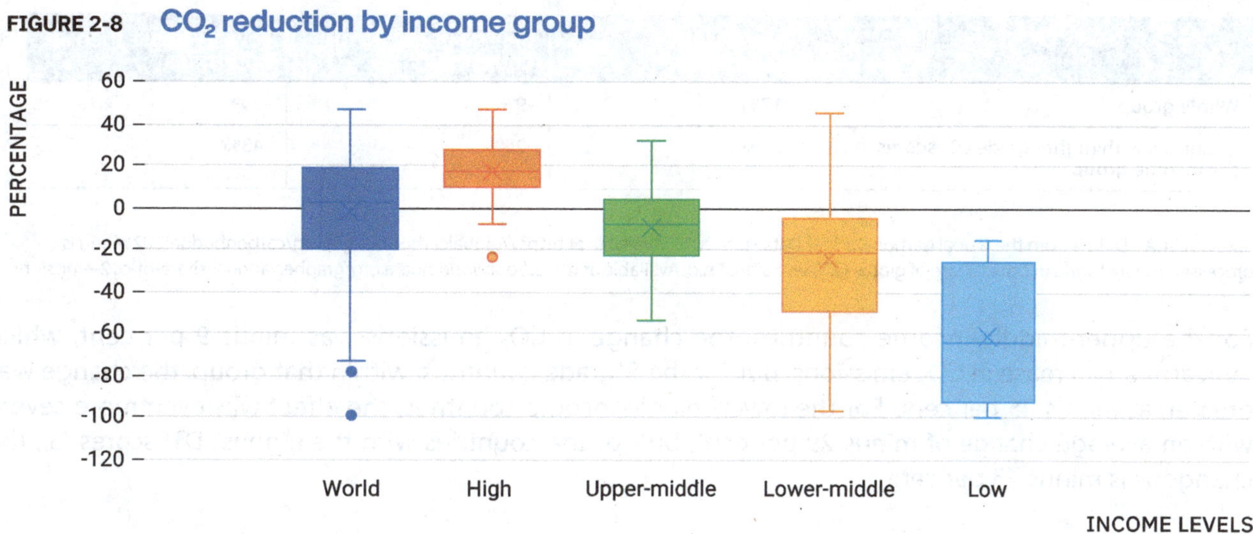

Source: Analysed by ESCAP. Data is from the Global Carbon Budget Data Hub, 2023. Available at https://globalcarbonbudget.org/carbonbudget2023/ and is processed by Our World in Data, "Share of global CO2 emissions", n.d. Available at https://ourworldindata.org/grapher/annual-share-of-co2-emissions

The pattern is similar when countries are grouped by DTI status (Figure 2-9), into five grades based on their DTI scores: S (above 80), A (above 60), B (above 40), C (above 20) and D (below 20). Figure 2-9 shows the mean DTI scores and the range of carbon emissions reduction for each of the DTI groups. While the mean values indicate the average rate of carbon emissions reduction, the ranges between the different DTI groups differ more; the variation in reduction rates is greatest for the countries in the C and D categories. This suggests that for countries with a lower levels of digital transformation, additional factors, apart from digital capacities, play a significant role resulting in more uneven progress.

FIGURE 2-9　　CO_2 reduction by Digital Transformation Index (DTI) category

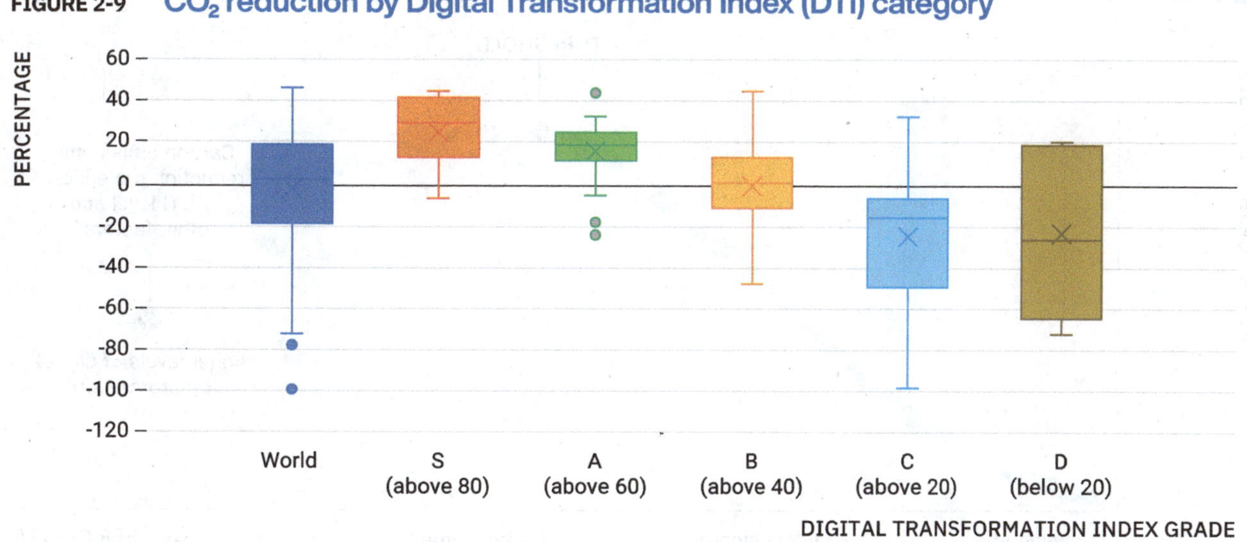

Source: Analysed by ESCAP. Data is from the Global Carbon Budget Data Hub, 2023. Available at https://globalcarbonbudget.org/carbonbudget2023/ and is processed by Our World in Data, "Share of global CO2 emissions", n.d. Available at https://ourworldindata.org/grapher/annual-share-of-co2-emissions

These connections are examined further in Table 2-1, which shows the CO_2 reduction rate (percentage) for each country income group, and also the change for the set of countries within that group which had the highest DTI scores (S). For the high-income countries, the average reduction was 17 per cent, but for the group of countries with the highest DTI scores (S) the reduction was 26 per cent. Even for countries with similar high incomes, higher digital transformation capacities and capabilities contributed to more effective CO_2 reduction.

TABLE 2-1   CO$_2$ reduction rate (%) by income group and by high Digital Transformation Index (DTI) score

	HIGH-INCOME COUNTRIES	UPPER-MIDDLE INCOME COUNTRIES	LOWER-MIDDLE INCOME COUNTRIES
Whole group	+17%	-9%	-29%
Countries with higher grade DTI scores in the income group	+26%	-25%	-43%

Source: ESCAP. Data is from the Global Carbon Budget Data Hub, 2023. Available at https://globalcarbonbudget.org/carbonbudget2023/ and is processed by Our World in Data, "Share of global CO2 emissions", n.d. Available at https://ourworldindata.org/grapher/annual-share-of-co2-emissions

For the upper-middle-income countries, the change in CO_2 emissions was minus 9 per cent, which indicates an increase in CO_2 emissions. But for the S-grade countries, within that group, the change was greater; at minus 25 per cent. For the lower-middle income countries, the effect was even more severe with an average change of minus 29 per cent, but for the countries with the highest DTI scores (S), the change was minus 43 per cent.

Once again, this suggests that for developing countries progress can be very uneven. While developed countries have undergone digital transformation after industrialization, developing countries are still undergoing digital transformation as they industrialize. In developing countries, structural transformation can thus outweigh the benefits of digital progress in contributing toward CO_2 reduction, and by a high margin.

Figure 2-10 illustrates a schematic picture with carbon emissions initially rising with per capita GDP, but beyond a certain threshold, with economic development, carbon emissions start to fall. This is the outcome of a combination of factors, such as the technological capacities, the implementation of deliberate policy and regulatory efforts, the nature of economic and social structures, and the sociocultural context. However, the reduction is likely to be steeper for countries with high levels of digital capacities.

FIGURE 2-10   Carbon emissions projection by income level and Digital Transformation Index (DTI) levels

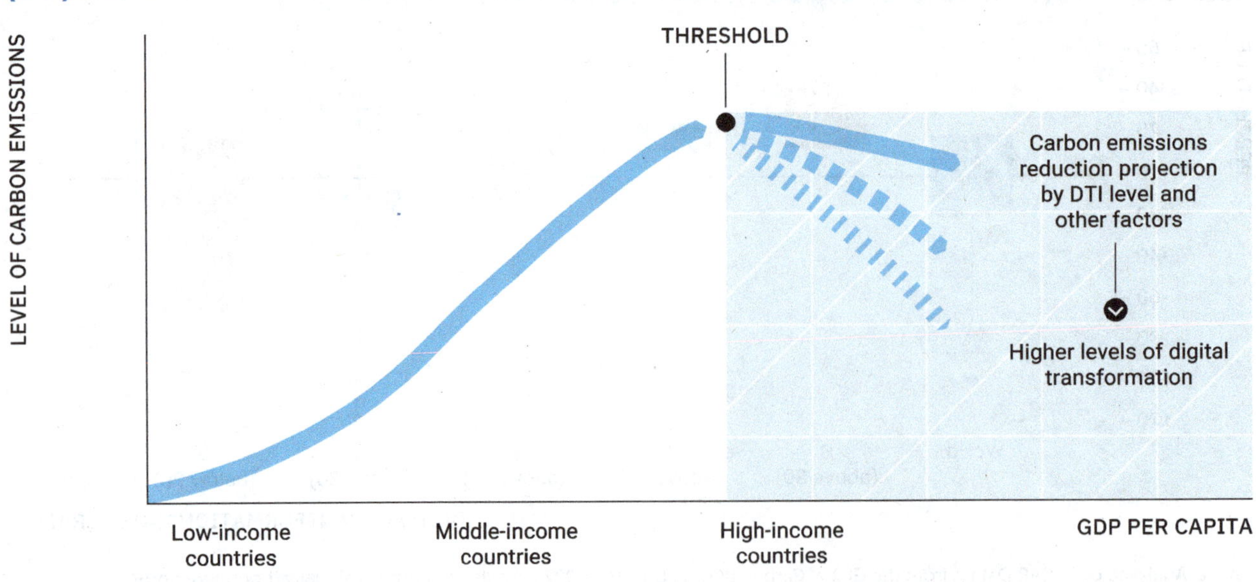

Source: ESCAP.

The carbon trajectory is influenced by technological development, offering a pathway to sustainable economic growth while addressing climate risks. However, the extent to which digital transformation contributes to climate action will depend on many other factors including the country's industrial and economic structure, its level of technological capacity and progress, sociocultural context, and deliberate country policies and actions.

2.2 Digital transformations align with energy transitions

The global energy system is undergoing a notable transformation, with a focus on a just, inclusive, and equitable energy transition based on renewables and energy efficiency. In pursuing a reduction of global carbon emissions to net zero by 2050, the transition from fossil fuels to renewable energy is imperative.

To assess progress in this direction, the World Economic Forum has developed the Energy Transition Index (ETI) which has two pillars (Figure 2-11). The first is system performance that is measured by equity, security and sustainability. The second is transition readiness which uses measures of regulatory policies, financial investment, talent development, infrastructure and technological innovation.

FIGURE 2-11 **The Energy Transition Index (ETI)**

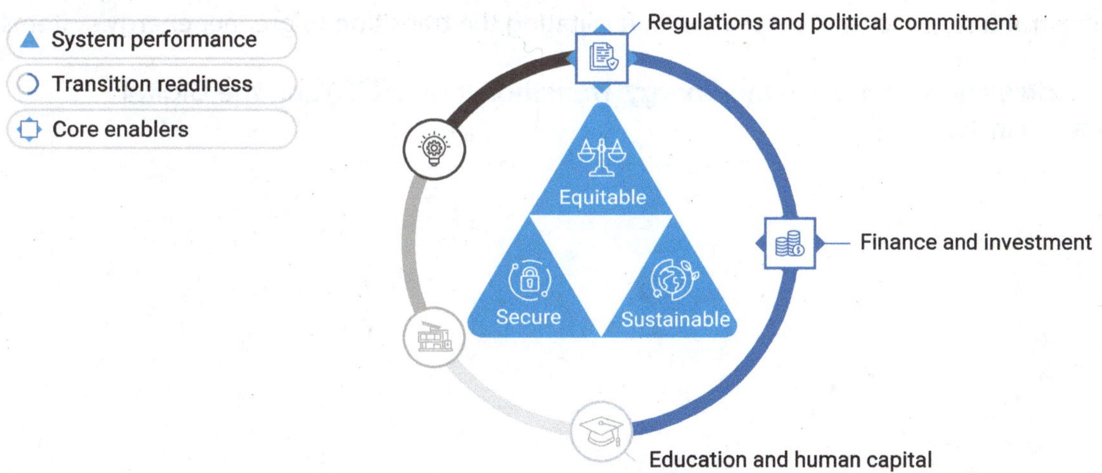

The ETI framework analyses countries' current energy system performance and enabling environment for energy transition in five equally weighted components: equity and inclusion, security, sustainability, regulatory framework and investment, and enabling factors.

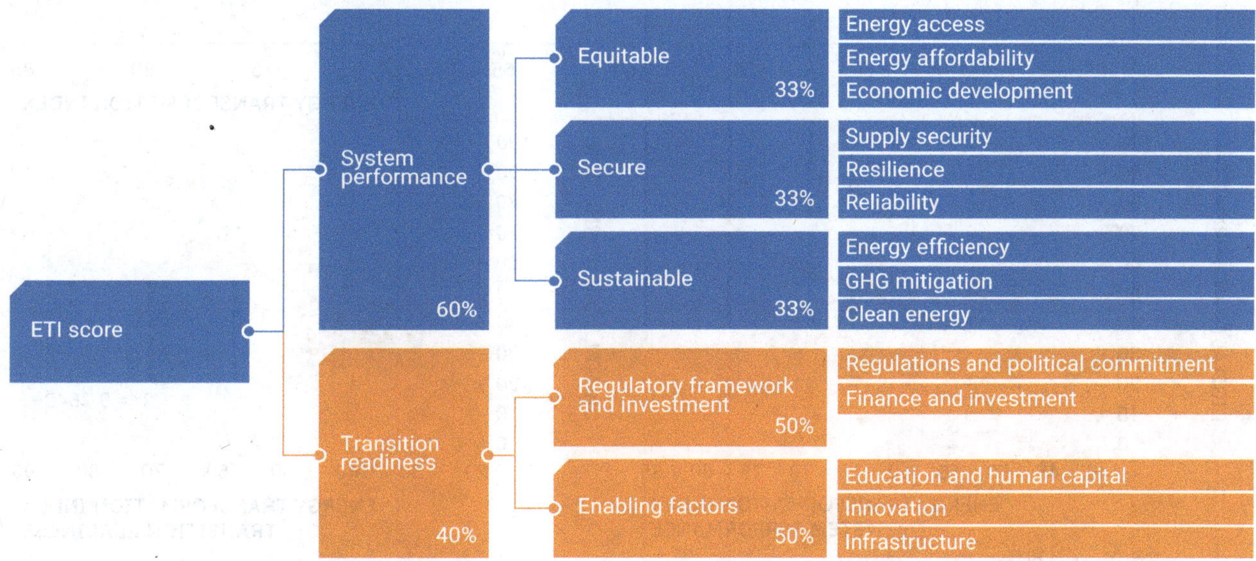

Source: World Economic Forum (WEF), "Fostering Effective Energy Transition 2023 edition", June. Available at https://www.weforum.org/reports/fostering-effective-energy-transition-2023/

Energy transition has important linkages with digital transformation. A higher capacity for digital transformation within a country can potentially indicate its capability to adopt digital tools and solutions for energy optimization, renewables integration, smart grids and energy transition efforts. Conversely, countries that lag in digital transformation may face challenges in fully embracing the opportunities that digitalization offers in the energy sector.

The ways in which the two align can be assessed by comparing the ETI with the DTI, to provide a multi-dimensional understanding of a sustainable digital and energy future, given the synergistic potential of these two critical domains in addressing climate change. As shown in Figure 2-12, the DTI is highly correlated with the Energy Transition Index's 'Transition Readiness' pillar (preparedness and enabling environment for green and smart energy transition), while the correlation with the 'System Performance' pillar (current energy system performance) is weaker. This indicates that a country's readiness to adopt and implement energy transition measures aligns more closely with its digital transformation status, emphasizing the influence of digital capabilities on the country's potential to transition towards sustainable energy practices.

This analysis can also be applied to groups of countries. Figure 2-13 shows the ETI performance by DTI countries grouped by their DTI status (S/A/B/C/D), and finds that countries with higher levels of digital capacities perform better on the ETI. The relationship between digital transformation and energy transition is shown to be synergistic. This comparative analysis therefore underscores the significance of digital infrastructure, policy and innovation in facilitating the transition to greener energy systems.

FIGURE 2-12 Correlations between the Energy Transition Index (ETI) and the Digital Transformation Index (DTI)

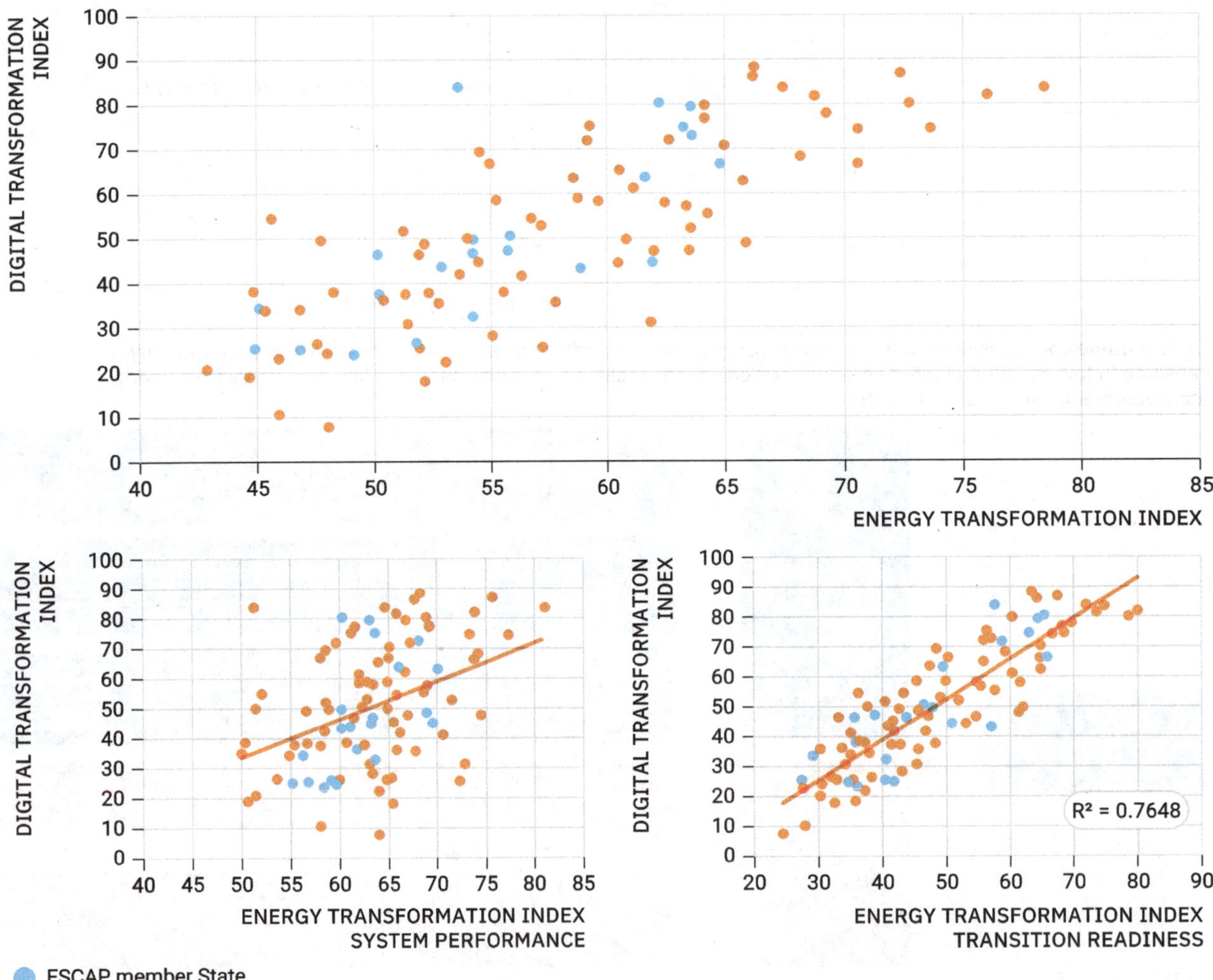

Source: Analysed by ESCAP. Data from World Economic Forum, "Energy Transition Index", 2024. Available at https://initiatives.weforum.org/energy-and-industry-transition-intelligence/energy-transition-index.

FIGURE 2-13 Energy Transition Index System Performance (ETI-SP) and Energy Transition Index Transition Readiness (ETI-TR) by Digital Transformation Index (DTI) Grades

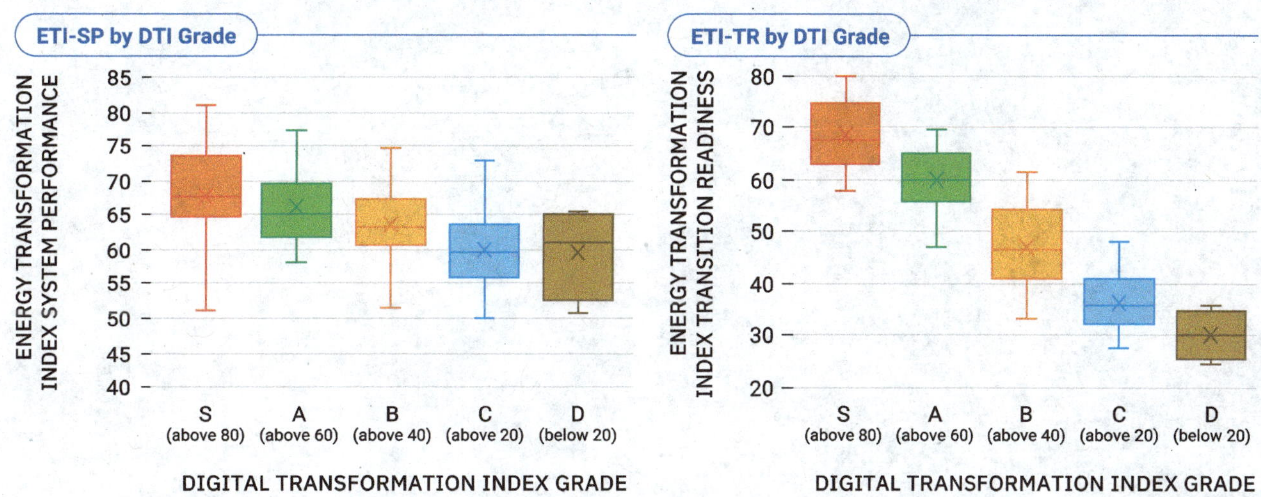

Source: Analysed by ESCAP. Data from World Economic Forum, "Energy Transition Index", 2024. Available at https://initiatives.weforum.org/energy-and-industry-transition-intelligence/energy-transition-index.

Digital transformations are helping to power countries to new levels of economic development, but the economic and social consequences depend on how digital tools are introduced and applied in practice, and with an eye to averting a climate catastrophe. The following chapter discusses digital applications that enhance climate action.

Chapter 2 References

Global Carbon Budget Data Hub (2023). Available at https://globalcarbonbudget.org/carbonbudget2023/

International Energy Agency (IEA) (2021). *Key World Energy Statistics 2021*. Paris. Available at https://www.iea.org/reports/key-world-energy-statistics-2021

__________ (2024a). CO_2 emissions from combustion in advanced economies, 1973–2023. 27 February. Available at https://www.iea.org/data-and-statistics/charts/co2-emissions-from-combustion-in-advanced-economies-1973-2023

__________ (2024b). *CO_2 Emissions in 2023*. Paris. Available at https://www.iea.org/reports/co2-emissions-in-2023

Jun, Seunghwa, Jongsur Park, and Jeong Yoon Kim (2022). Digital transformation landscape in Asia and the Pacific: Aggravated digital divide and widening growth gap. United Nations Economic and Social Commission for Asia and the Pacific (ESCAP), Information and Communications Technology and Disaster Risk Reduction Division. Working Paper Series. July. Bangkok. Available at https://www.unescap.org/kp/2022/digital-transformation-landscape-asia-and-pacific-aggravated-digital-divide-and-widening

Our World in Data (n.d.). Share of global CO_2 emissions. Available at https://ourworldindata.org/grapher/annual-share-of-co2-emissions

Ritchie, Hannah, Pablo Rosado and Max Roser (2023). CO_2 and greenhouse gas emissions. Our World in Data. Available at https://ourworldindata.org/co2-and-greenhouse-gas-emissions

Stern, David, I. (2004). Environmental Kuznets Curve. In *Encyclopedia of Energy*, Cutler J. Cleveland, ed. Elsevier. Available at https://www.sciencedirect.com/topics/earth-and-planetary-sciences/environmental-kuznets-curve

United Nations (n.d.). Renewable energy – powering a safer future. Available at https://www.un.org/en/climatechange/raising-ambition/renewable-energy

United Nations Environment Programme (UNEP) (n.d.). Global Material Flows Database. Available at https://www.resourcepanel.org/global-material-flows-database

World Economic Forum (WEF) (2023). *Fostering Effective Energy Transition 2023 edition*. June. Available at https://www.weforum.org/reports/fostering-effective-energy-transition-2023/

World Economic Forum (2024). Energy Transition Index. Available at https://initiatives.weforum.org/energy-and-industry-transition-intelligence/energy-transition-index

CHAPTER 3

Digital applications
for climate action

Digital technologies are game changers, not just for achieving economic growth, but also for addressing climate change. Artificial intelligence, machine learning, the Internet of Things, digital twins, cloud-enabled tools and other emerging technologies are helping to scale up innovations and solutions, even in the hardest-to-abate sectors, that can boost efficiency, optimize energy infrastructure and reduce carbon emissions.

Digital tools are also critical for adaptation. Advanced analytics and geospatial technologies, for example, are helping countries respond to increasingly frequent and more severe climate-induced natural disasters. This chapter offers case studies and good practices of digital applications for climate action, that range across infrastructure, governance, mobility, industry and trade, disaster risk reduction, and agriculture and biodiversity ecosystems.

3.1 Smart infrastructure

Infrastructure is responsible for an estimated 79 per cent of all GHG emissions and 88 per cent of adaptation costs (UNEP, 2021). Thus, smarter infrastructure that has lower emissions and consumes less energy can make an important contribution to climate action.

Fortunately, in many countries, infrastructure is becoming steadily smarter in the ways it is built, managed and delivered, and through full life cycles, from design, construction, operation and management to the reuse of infrastructure waste.

When incorporated into buildings or roads or bridges, for example, digital technologies can gather and analyse data and detect early signs of deterioration, optimize maintenance schedules, and find corrective solutions to prevent unexpected faults. This allows installations to respond to any shocks, maintain functionality and minimize negative impacts (Figure 3-1). As a result, compared with traditional infrastructure, smarter installations are more resilient and better able to anticipate, prepare for, and adapt to changing climate conditions, and to cope with climate-related and other natural disasters, such as earthquakes, typhoons and floods (ESCAP, 2023a).

FIGURE 3-1 **How digital technologies can improve climate resilience of infrastructure**

PHASE OF RESILIENCE	TRADITIONAL MANAGEMENT RAMIFICATIONS	EMERGING TECHNOLOGIES ENHANCING DIFFERENT PHASES OF THE LIFE CYCLE CLIMATE RESILIENCE		
		EMERGING DIGITAL TECHNOLOGY	5G • internet of Things (IoT) • structural health monitoring (SHM)	RESILIENCE ENHANCEMENT - EXAMPLE
A Plan prepare	Climate change leading to decrease of performance • reduced knowledge of ageing, accelerated deterioration, increadsed demand	Building information modelling (BIM) • digital twins • digital analytics • machine learning and artificial intelligence (AI) • agent-based modelling		Climate preparedness, including the impact of multiple stressors • better understanding of interdependcies • accurate evaluation of infrastructure exposure • update of hazard models
B Absorb respond	Excessive losses due to inadequate preparedness and high vulnerabilities	Phone metadata • crowdsourcing • social media • data analytics • unmanned aerial vehicle (UAV) • light detection and ranging (LiDAR)		Reduced losses due to early warnings or monitoring of interoperabilities
C Recover	Delayed commencement of recovery due to uncertainties in understanding asset condition • slow recovery due to inefficient prioritization and allocation of resources	UAV • LiDAR • satellites • aerial imagery • machine learning & AI		Smaller idle time due to rapid post-disaster assessment • fast recovery by guiding response • drones using machine learning for damage detection
D Adapt	Inadequate information for asset performance and interdependences • subjective allocation of resources	agent-based modelling • augmented and mixed reality • sensors from connected vehicles		Data-driven adaptation enhanced by innovative/sustainable solutions • monitoring of infrastructural, technological, social, informational and environmental interdependices • prevent cascading threats

Source: Sotirios A. Argyroudis, and others, "Digital technologies can enhance climate resilience of critical infrastructure", *Climate Risk Management*, vol. 35 (2022). Available at https://www.sciencedirect.com/science/article/pii/S2212096321001169

Optimizing energy infrastructure through smart grids

Many of these benefits derive from optimizing energy infrastructures which helps emerging economies to leapfrog some of the energy transition challenges faced by large and centralized and even aging energy infrastructures. Smart energy grids are the electrical power networks which integrates digital technologies, big data analytics and emerging renewable energy. Smart grid systems that have multi-directional energy flow and power transmission can respond to sudden surges in demand and automatically reroute electricity flows (Figure 3-2). In China, for example, it has been estimated that applying smart grids can reduce carbon emissions from manufacturing industry by 27.51 per cent, in optimal scenarios (Fu, Shi, and Zeng, 2021).

FIGURE 3-2   **Smart energy grid system**

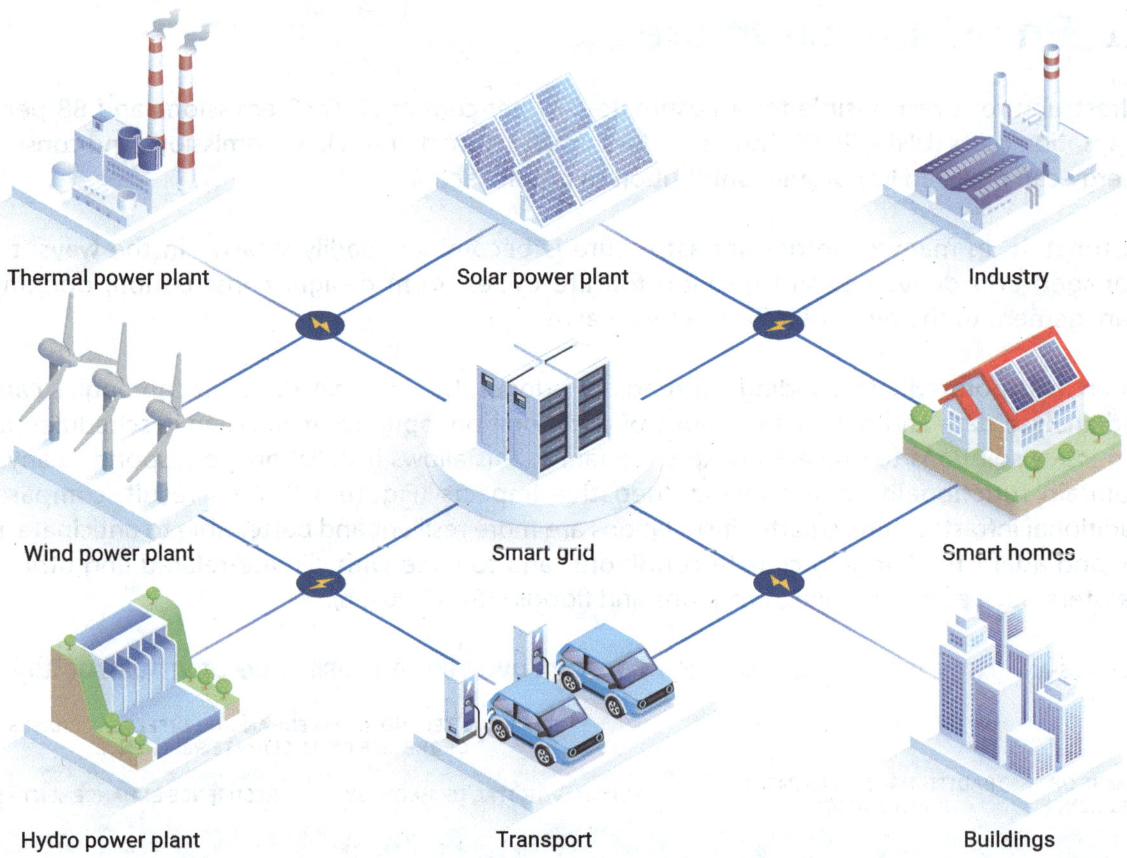

Source: International Energy Agency (IEA) , "Digitalization & Energy", Webinar, 7 February 2018. Available at https://iea.blob.core.windows.net/assets/e5ffa993-ef78-49f7-8cfa-5375a41d074e/ieadigitalizationandenergywebinar-180220161419.pdf

AI-driven smart grids can also optimize supply and demand and facilitate the integration of renewables (United Nations, 2023). This helps reduce waste and improves grid stability, which minimizes carbon emissions and environmental damage.

Similar benefits can be achieved in other infrastructure such as buildings. Modern grid-interactive buildings typically incorporate solar generation with battery storage, smart windows and shading, computer-controlled heating and lighting and many other technologies (Box 3-1). Moreover, the benefits can be extended to entire urban areas that embrace multiple types of smart infrastructure, from transport, to water supplies, to waste disposal, resulting in new forms of smart infrastructure (Box 3-2).

BOX 3.1   Efficient grid-interactive buildings in the United States of America

Over the next two decades, in the United States of America, the adoption of efficient grid-interactive buildings (EGIBs) could reduce power system costs nationwide by between $100 billion and $200 billion.[a] By 2030, EGIBs could reduce CO_2 annual emissions by 6 per cent, which amounts to about 80 million tons.[b] There would also be significant savings in energy, ranging from 164 TWh to 401 TWh.[c] Demand savings would range from 42 GW to 116 GW depending on the adoption of various grid-interactive solutions.[d]

Efficient grid-interactive buildings

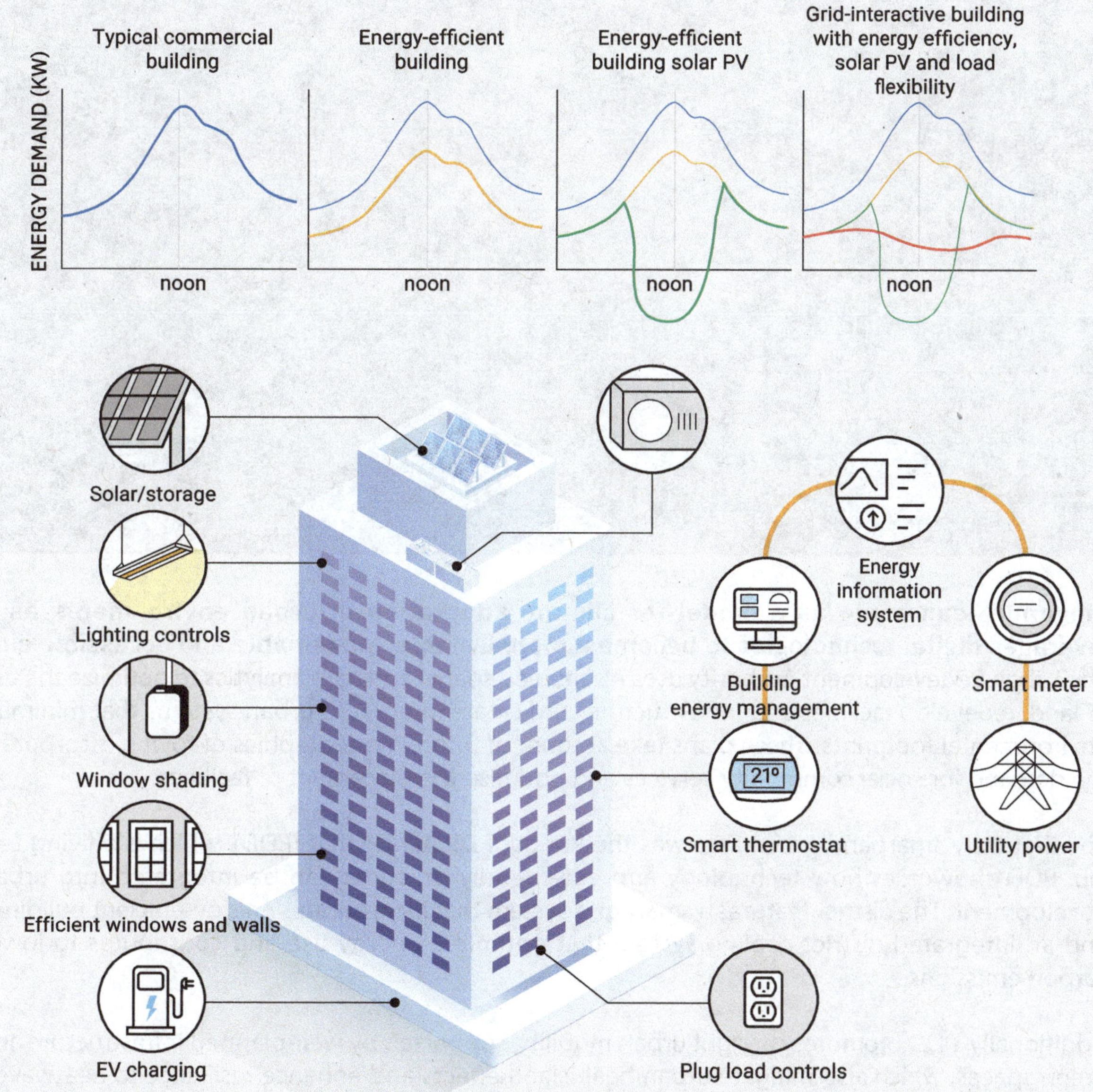

Source: International Energy Agency (IEA), "Unlocking the potential of distributed energy resources: Power system opportunities and best practices", n.d.c. Available at https://iea.blob.core.windows.net/assets/3520710c-c828-4001-911c-ae78b645ce67/UnlockingthePotentialofDERs_Powersystemopportunitiesandbestpractices.pdf

a   International Energy Agency (IEA), "Efficient Grid-Interactive Buildings: Future of buildings in ASEAN", n.d.a. Available at https://iea.blob.core.windows.net/assets/71d1b69d-e8aa-49e5-9e0c-12c13d5a3a1f/EfficientGrid-InteractiveBuildings.pdf
b   Ibid.
c   Ibid.
d   Ibid.

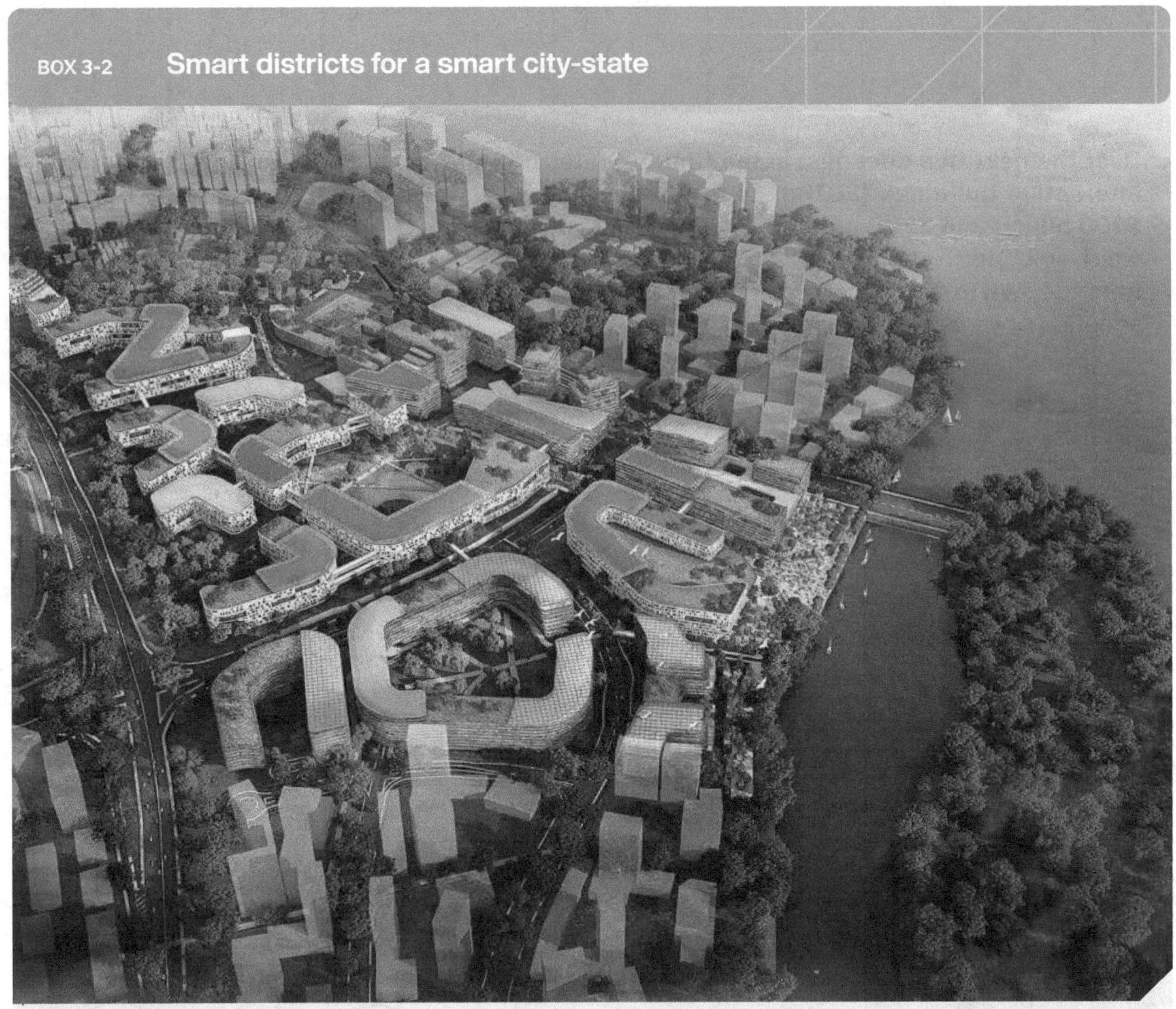

Singapore can serve as a model for climate adaptation in urban environments as it leverages digital technologies to become a more liveable, sustainable and accessible city. The Urban Redevelopment Authority uses AI-enabled spatial and data analytics to optimize the use of land, redevelop facilities and infrastructure, and create integrated urban systems that minimize environmental footprints. These plans take account of future demographics of towns, incorporate the demand for social community services and optimize the placement of facilities.

The first truly smart and green area was the Punggol Digital District (PDD), which is a living test lab. PDD showcases how technology and eco-friendly practices can be integrated into urban development. The district features a smart grid system that incorporates energy-efficient buildings and an integrated district cooling system that optimizes energy use and contributes to lower carbon emissions.

Additionally, PDD promotes car-light urban mobility, supported by well-planned infrastructure and green spaces, which also mitigate urban heat island effects and enhance resilience to heatwaves. Smart technologies also reduce water consumption and waste generation.

Sources:

Huang Zhongwen, "AI in Urban Planning: 3 ways it will strengthen how we plan for the future", Urban Redevelopment Authority, 1 September 2021. Available at https://www.ura.gov.sg/Corporate/Resources/Ideas-and-Trends/AI-in-Urban-Planning

Urban Redevelopment Authority, "Urban Transformations: Punggol Digital District", 2024. Available at https://www.ura.gov.sg/Corporate/Planning/Master-Plan/Master-Plan-2019/Urban-Transformations/Punggol-Digital-District

Photo: Urban Redevelopment Authority

Digital twins for climate-resilient infrastructure

A digital twin is a virtual representation, a digital model, of a physical object, system, or process (IBM, n.d.). Compared with standard simulations, digital twins offer far more vantage points. Researchers and planners can use the digital twin to test out new ideas or to see how multiple components of a system might respond and interact in real time, and discover ways to improve the original. Digital twins can thus help countries try different climate adaptation and mitigation strategies before they are undertaken.

Digital twins are being used for climate modelling and for tracking and predicting changes in the patterns of the Earth's systems, notably the atmosphere and oceans (Gent, 2021). Nvidia's Earth-2 (Gent, 2021), and the Destination Earth initiative (Destination Earth, n.d.), for example, use the most advanced methods to model climate change. They are providing important projections and insights on mitigation and adaptation.

Digital twins can also be used for managing energy infrastructure and for optimizing the energy efficiency of buildings, infrastructures and engines, including wind turbines or even entire cities. By identifying inefficiencies in building systems, digital twins can signal more energy-efficient options. For example, they can improve indoor air quality, reduce energy usage, or produce less waste, and generally shrink the carbon footprint. Research by Ernest and Young Global Limited estimates that digital twins can reduce GHG emissions and the carbon footprint of an existing building by up to 50 per cent, including by measuring the optimized models on energy usage, reducing waste, and improving indoor air quality within the building (Sáiz, 2022; Frearson, 2021). Multiple twins of different components of urban life can also be combined to model the behaviour of an entire city (Box 3-3).

<table>
<tr><td>BOX 3-3</td><td>Virtual Singapore and Cooling Singapore Initiatives</td></tr>
</table>

Virtual Singapore is a comprehensive digital twin of the city-state. The platform allows city planners, working with different government agencies, to create rich visual models of Singapore that they can use to run simulations, derive insights, develop solutions and boost urban resilience.

This platform can be used to assess and predict the impact of climate change on infrastructure, such as the effects of rising temperatures and increased flooding on buildings and transportation networks, thus informing both mitigation and adaptation strategies. Virtual Singapore also enhances disaster preparedness by allowing simulation of flooding, thereby guiding the development of pre-emptive actions.

Another project using a specialized digital twin is 'Cooling Singapore 2.0', which addresses steadily rising temperatures. This digital urban twin integrates various computational models; environmental, land surface, industrial, traffic, and building energy, and can be used to carry out experiments, explore scenarios, and develop climate-responsive design guidelines for application at both district and island scales.

Sources:

Geospatial.SG (n.d.). Virtual Singapore. Available at https://www.sla.gov.sg/geospatial/gw/virtual-singapore

Juan A. Acero, and Ander Zozaya, "Cooling Singapore: Digital Urban Climate Twin (DUCT), n.d. Available at https://www.thegpsc.org/sites/gpsc/files/cooling_singapore_-_digital_urban_climate_twin.pdf

National University of Singapore, "Cooling Singapore 2.0 – Digital Urban Climate Twin", 8 January 2024. Available at https://fass.nus.edu.sg/srn/2024/01/08/cooling-singapore-2-0-digital-urban-climate-twin/

Smart waste management

Climate change is being exacerbated by emissions from millions of tons of garbage. After agriculture and fossil fuels, the waste sector is the world's third-largest source of methane emissions, which are responsible for about 20 per cent of the total global anthropogenic emissions (UNEP and Climate and Clean Air Coalition, 2021).

Digital innovations can cut emissions by making waste management more efficient, improving rates of recycling and creating circular processes (GSMA, 2024). For example, in the United States of America, the North Carolina State University, the U.S. National Renewable Energy Laboratory and IBM are collaborating on a smart waste management system (Moore, 2023). This includes an automated waste sorting machine that incorporates smart sensors, and visual and hyperspectral cameras that examine the physical, chemical and biological properties of non-recyclable waste items to determine their contaminants, energy density, and organic content.

Of particular concern is waste that leaks into rivers and oceans, including plastic bags or bottles, that can litter beaches across the region and that can break down into microplastics that are detrimental to human and animal health. In partnership with the Government of Japan, ESCAP's 'Closing the Loop' project supported governments by leveraging innovative technologies to address plastic waste pollution and leakages into the marine environment (Box 3-4).

In South-East Asia, around 75 per cent of land-based sources of marine plastic pollution originate from uncollected waste, and 25 per cent from leakages in municipal waste management systems. Plastic pollution is also transboundary; up to 95 per cent of plastics in the world's oceans is transported by ten major rivers, eight of which are in Asia.

ESCAP, in partnership with the Government of Japan, has implemented the 'Closing the Loop' project which uses innovative technologies to reduce plastic waste pollution and leakages into the marine environment. The project has supported four ASEAN cities: Kuala Lumpur, Malaysia; Surabaya, Indonesia; Nakhon Si Thammarat, Thailand; and Da Nang, Viet Nam. By using remote sensing, satellites and crowdsourced data applications, the project can detect and monitor the sources and pathways of plastic waste entering rivers in urban catchment areas.

The project is producing plastic waste maps and simulations for each pilot city and is training officials and stakeholders in ASEAN cities to use smart technologies to monitor, assess, report on, and sustainably manage plastic waste as well as further strengthen municipal solid waste management systems.

Source: United Nations Economic and Social Commission for Asia and the Pacific (ESCAP), "New UN initiative to reduce plastic pollution from ASEAN cities", press release, 5 May 2020. Available at https://www.unescap.org/news/new-un-initiative-reduce-plastic-pollution-asean-cities

Photo: Naja Bertolt Jensen

BOX 3-5   **RFID-based food waste management in the Republic of Korea**

In 2010, the Republic of Korea initiated a programme for tracking household food waste. This uses radio frequency identification (RFID) tags attached to waste bins. RFID tags are smart labels that can store a range of information including serial numbers linked to each household.

Seoul Metropolitan Government, in conjunction with SK Telecom, has implemented the system which automatically measures the amount of food waste and charges each household the appropriate disposal fee. This has encouraged citizens to reduce and recycle food waste.

RFID food waste management system

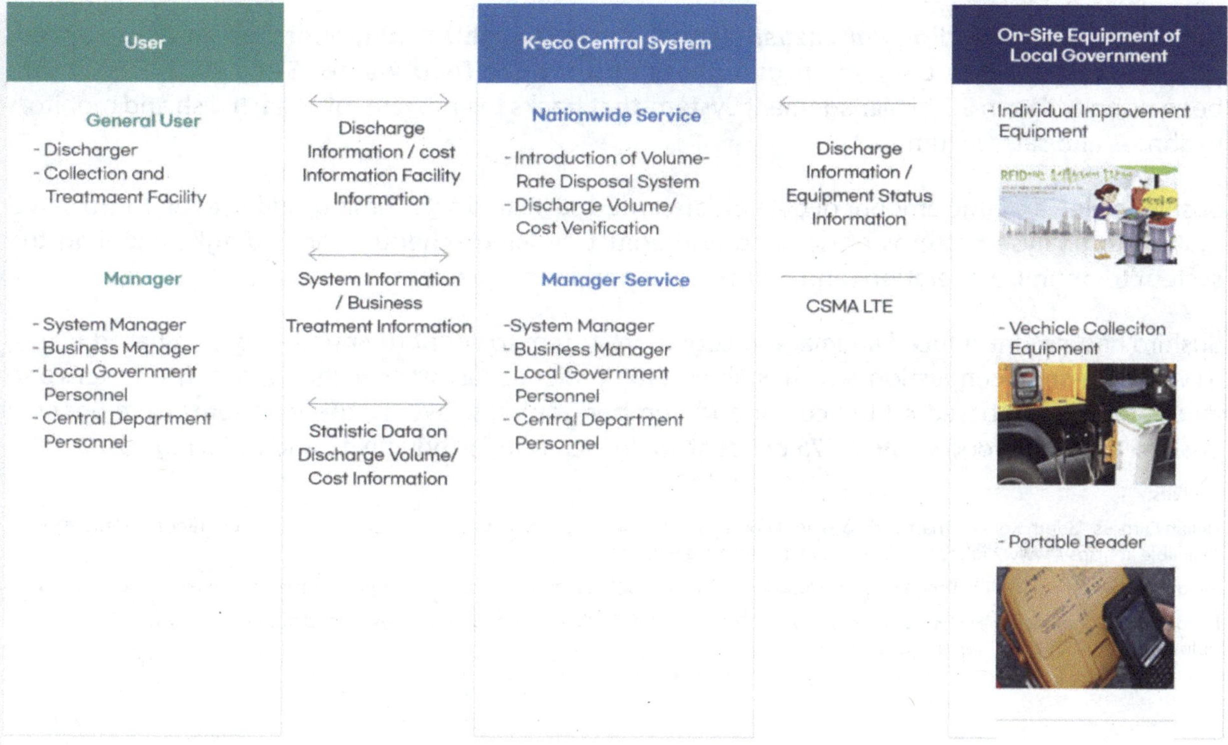

In 2016, the system reduced restaurant food waste in Seoul by 40 per cent and household food waste by 30 per cent. From 2021, the Republic of Korea broadened the usage of RFID in tracking other sources of foods, such as fish and beef.

Sources:

Karim Chrobog, "South Korea: Cutting Back on Food Waste", Pulitzer Center, 12 November 2015. Available at https://pulitzercenter.org/stories/south-korea-cutting-back-food-waste

Korea Environment Corporation, "RFID-based food wastes management system", 2023. Available at https://www.keco.or.kr/en/lay1/S295T387C404/contents.do

Leon Kaye, "Swipe card technology introduced for food waste bins", *The Guardian*, 26 January 2012. Available at https://www.theguardian.com/sustainable-business/south-korea-swipe-card-food-waste

RFID World, "South Korea: Wastage of food reduced using RFID", 12 July 2024. Available at https://rfidworld.ca/south-korea-wastage-of-food-reduced-using-rfid

United Nations Economic and Social Commission for Asia and the Pacific (ESCAP), "New UN initiative to reduce plastic pollution from ASEAN cities", press release, 5 May 2020. Available at https://www.unescap.org/news/new-un-initiative-reduce-plastic-pollution-asean-cities

Waste should also be used to generate energy. The methane from landfills can be piped away for combustion to be fed into national gas grids. Non-recyclable waste materials, such as oil, grease, and dirt, can be transformed into energy and fuel. Here, too, AI can assist. In China, for example, 100 waste incineration plants in 30 cities, which accounts for 10 per cent of the total, are using AI and Alibaba Cloud to analyse images of the flames inside the furnace. A Korean company, SK ecoplant and Amazon Web Services (AWS) built an AI incinerator solution, using the cloud's machine learning to enhance efficiency and reduce pollutants emission (APN News, 2021). Based on the shape of the flames, an AI algorithm detects incomplete combustion and automatically adjusts parameters, such as temperature and levels of oxygen and steam, in real time to keep the incinerator at optimal efficiency, reduce toxic emissions and maximize energy output (Yu, 2022).

BOX 3-6   **An AI-driven sushi management system in Japan**

Sushiro, Japan's leading *kaitenzushi* (conveyor-belt sushi) chain, operates an AI-powered, predictive system to enhance productivity and reduce food waste. Since 2002, Sushiro has been using a 'Kaiten Sushi Management System' that tracks the movement of each dish and monitors freshness and sales volume.

Sushiro collects a large amount of data on discarded sushi and sales timing, and uses an AI-powered system to analyse patterns of demand and adjust cooking schedules accordingly, enabling the system to optimize operations and reduce costs and food waste.

Sushiro has also introduced an image-recognition system to count the number of purchased plates, as well as in-store congestion, which enables it to predict to customer waiting times. The system also calculates the bill based on the colour and number of plates. Overall, these systems have enabled Sushiro to reduce food waste by 75 per cent while increasing productivity and reducing costs.

Sources:

Dyllan Furness, "South Korea's smart garbage cans know how much waste you toss and charge accordingly", Digital Trends, 10 May 2016. Available at https://www.digitaltrends.com/home/south-korea-waste/

Food and Life Companies, "Challenge to reduce food loss with DX", n.d. Available at https://food-and-life.co.jp/en/sustainability/sushisystem/

Food and Life Companies, "Sustainability Report 2023", 22 December 2023. Available at https://www.food-and-life.co.jp/wp-content/uploads/pdf/sustainability/report2023.pdf

---

3.2 Digital government for climate action

Governments across Asia and the Pacific are using digital tools and platforms to improve the quality and efficiency of public operations, while also widening access to both services and information, and increasing accountability through greater transparency and opportunities for citizen participation.

Governments can take advantage of new technologies to improve efficiency, optimize infrastructure and facilitate remote services. More accessible public services can also help businesses, start-ups and entrepreneurs to play their part, for example, with easier systems for applying for licenses to invest in climate-related sectors (UNCTAD, 2023). Governments can extend education and capacity-building to encourage community engagement in climate action.

Digital identification (IDs) to support climate action

As of 2022, 8 out of 10 ASEAN member States had implemented, or were planning to implement, national digital ID systems (GovInsider, 2024). Singapore's Singpass, for example, first launched in 2003, provides residents with a trusted digital identity for easy and secure access to over 2,000 government and private-sector services.

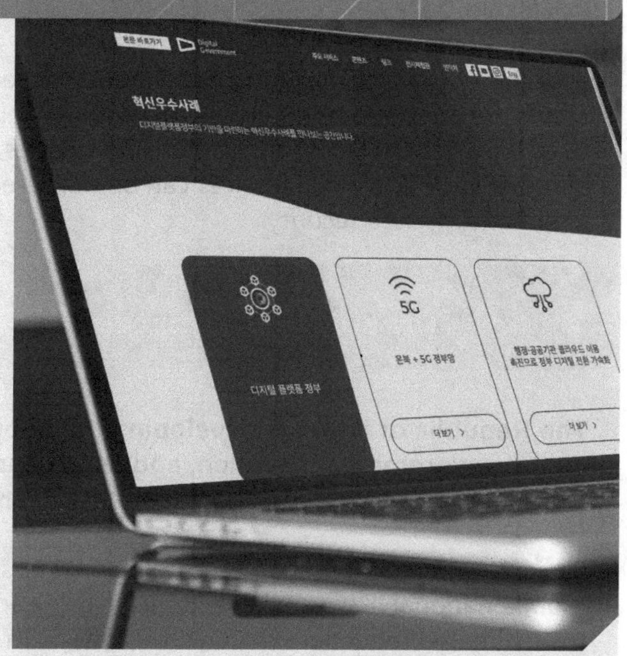

BOX 3-7   Digital Platform Government in the Republic of Korea

In 2020, the Republic of Korea pledged to achieve carbon neutrality by 2050. The 2050 Carbon Neutral Strategy Action Plan involves setting up a low-carbon economic structure and developing core technologies for low-carbon industries, while also creating the necessary institutions for a fair transition to a carbon-neutral society.

In 2022, this was supplemented with Digital Platform Government. This AI- and cloud-based platform enables citizens, businesses and government to collaborate. Digital technologies can contribute to people-centred, transparent and science-based governance that also helps drive private-sector growth.

Sources:

Koh Jean, "Korea's new innovation strategy: Digital Platform Government", World Economic Forum, 13 January 2023. Available at https://www.weforum.org/agenda/2023/01/davos23-korea-digital-platform-government/

President Commission on Carbon Neutrality and Green Growth, "2050 Carbon Neutrality of the Republic of Korea", n.d. Available at https://www.2050cnc.go.kr/eng/main/view

The Government of the Republic of Korea, "2050 Carbon Neutral Strategy of the Republic of Korea: Towards a sustainable and green society", December 2020. Available at https://unfccc.int/sites/default/files/resource/LTS1_RKorea.pdf

Digital identification systems eliminate paper- and-plastic-based IDs whose production, transportation and storage creates large volumes of carbon emissions. With IDs, citizens no longer need to travel to government offices to access official services that require identity verification, such as social security or taxation, or to the offices of commercial services, such as banks. Eliminating physical transactions across Asia and the Pacific could cut millions of kilogrammes of CO_2 emissions each year.

Digital IDs can also boost climate adaptive capacity. By linking digital IDs to geographic and demographic data, governments and organizations can accurately identify and target populations vulnerable to the impacts of climate change. In addition, digital IDs can facilitate access to public services for climate adaptation, enhance disaster response and recovery, and support prompt data-driven decision-making on the vulnerabilities and adaptation needs of affected populations.

Digital IDs for disaster and humanitarian response

Digital solutions can enable governments and communities to better prepare for disasters resulting from climate shocks and extreme weather events. Notably, the data generated by such digital IDs not only allows governments to identify those most in need of income support pre-disaster, but it also enables disbursement of social protection payments in a more targeted and quicker way, thus providing a critical means of post-disaster coping and recovery. Furthermore, during disasters, rescue teams and relief agencies can more easily verify the identities of affected individuals and provide necessary services.

UNHCR, for example, has implemented digital ID systems to help ensure that refugees and internally displaced or stateless persons can access assistance and protection services during pandemics or other crises (Sköld, 2021).

If governments are to maximize the benefits for service delivery, they will need to ensure that the data systems are inter-operable across organizations related to humanitarian, health care and social care, as well as banks and telecommunications companies, and enable secure information-sharing. In this way, a range of socioeconomic services can be delivered in a coordinated manner while protecting privacy and enhancing data security.

BOX 3-8	The K-DID platform reduces CO_2 emissions in the Republic of Korea

The Republic of Korea is developing its mobile ID platform (K-DID) as a core project of its digital government innovation, and as a means of improving public services, building social trust, and strengthening citizens' rights over their private information.

Since 2021, the system has been rolled out in stages and will culminate, by 2025, in the issue of mobile national IDs, mobile residence cards and mobile welfare cards. The chart below indicates the estimated reductions in CO_2 emissions, with most of the benefits coming from the elimination of plastic ID cards.[a]

Estimated reduction in CO_2 emissions from use of the K-DID system

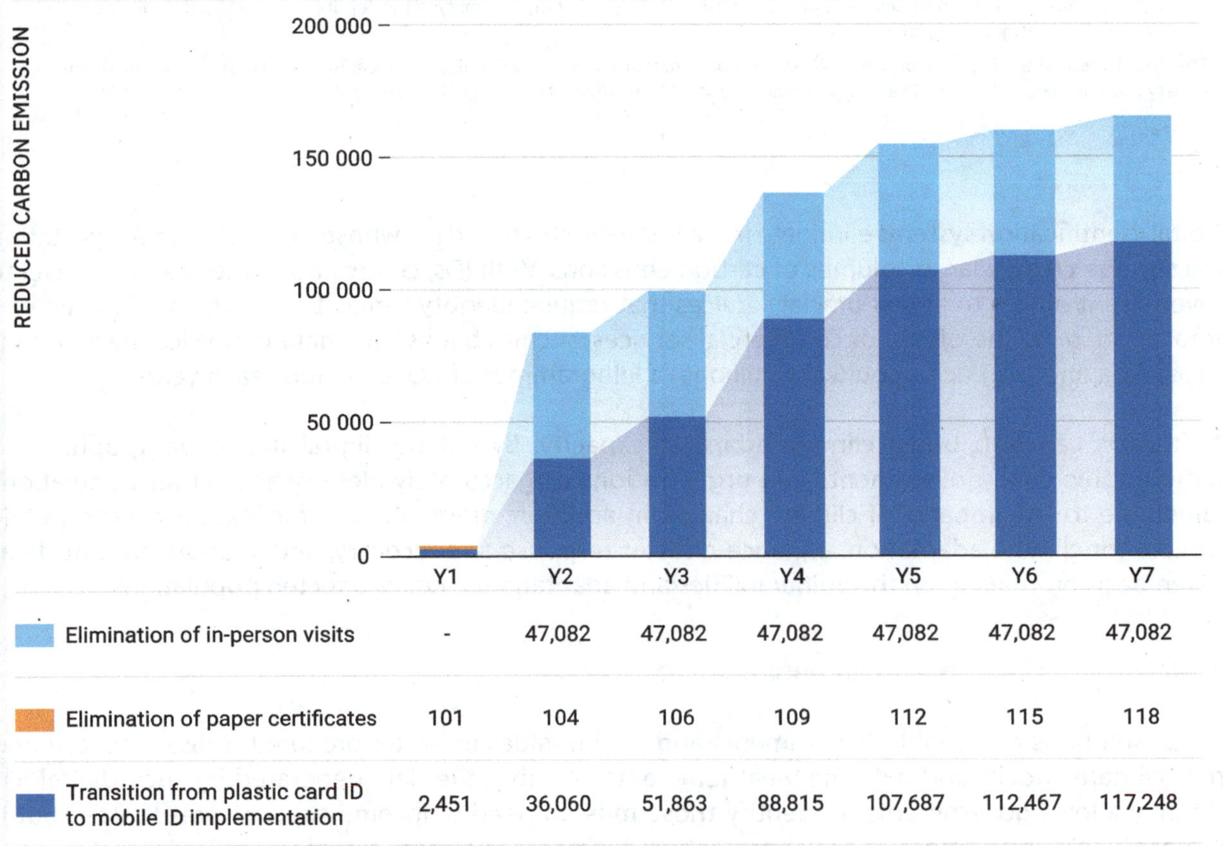

	Y1	Y2	Y3	Y4	Y5	Y6	Y7
Elimination of in-person visits	-	47,082	47,082	47,082	47,082	47,082	47,082
Elimination of paper certificates	101	104	106	109	112	115	118
Transition from plastic card ID to mobile ID implementation	2,451	36,060	51,863	88,815	107,687	112,467	117,248

Source: Shared by KOMSCO partners as input to this *Report*.

a KOMSCO, "Mobile ID (K-DID)", 2019. Available at https://www.komsco.com/eng/contents/166

3.3 Smart transport

In Asia and the Pacific, the transport sector contributes around one-quarter of GHG emissions, which is higher than the global average that is around one-fifth (World Bank, 2024). Transport also accounts for more than half of the region's total fossil fuel consumption.

Despite technological advances and low-carbon measures, these emissions continue to grow. Without more ambitious action, both transport demand and CO_2 emissions in the region could increase by more than 50 per cent by 2050 (ESCAP, 2023c).

This outcome could be avoided by taking greater advantage of digital transformations, which could reduce global GHG gas emissions by 5 per cent by 2050 (George, O'Regan, and Holst, 2022). Innovations can include electric vehicles and ride-sharing schemes and other equipment and services that take full advantage of satellite navigation, AI, IoT, cloud computing, edge computing and 5G telecommunications (ESCAP, 2023b).

<table>
<tr><td>BOX 3-9</td><td>Big data optimizes bus routes in Seoul, the Republic of Korea</td></tr>
</table>

Officials in Seoul, the Republic of Korea, wished to expand their transport network to include night-time bus routes. To gauge the demand and better understand the movements of night-time travellers they reached out to a major telecommunications provider which was able to collect and analyse 3 billion mobile anonymous phone logs. These data were overlaid on the map of Seoul to show the movements of the late-night population, which then informed the design of new bus routes and timetables for the 'Owl Bus' system.

Seoul's 'Owl Bus' system is creating strong incentives for its citizens to use the extended night-time public transport network and is estimated to have eliminated over 50,000 tons of carbon dioxide.

Travel data overlaid on the map of Seoul, left and Current Owl Bus routes, right

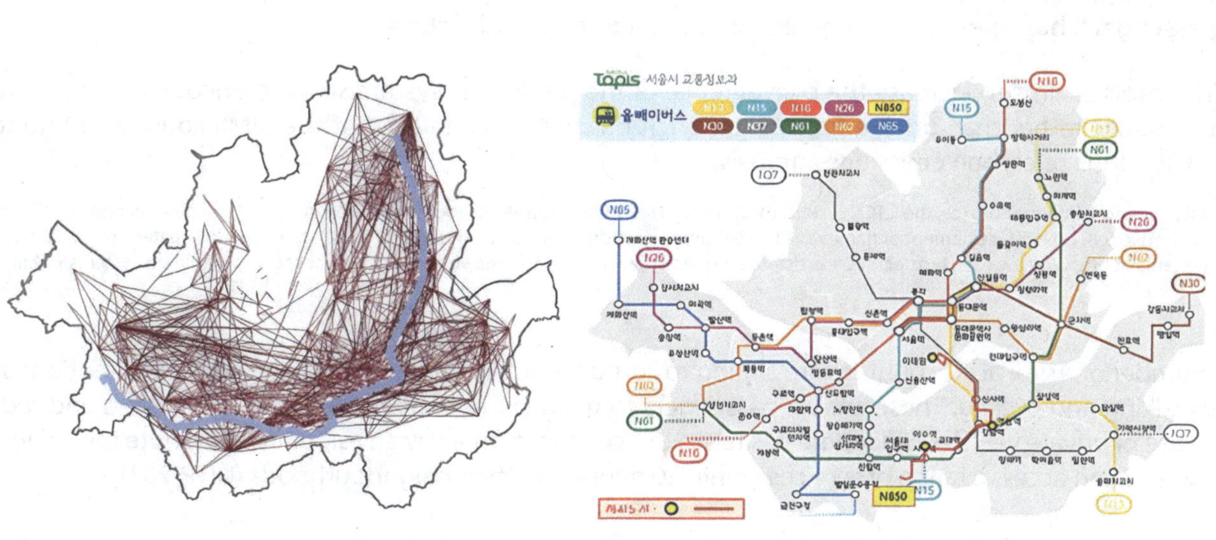

Source: Seoul Metropolitan Government, "Travel safely around the city even at night with Seoul's "Owl Bus"", 22 December 2016. Available at https://english.seoul.go.kr/travel-safely-around-city-even-night-seouls-owl-bus/

Connecting transport modes

Transport networks become much more efficient and attractive to users if they are well integrated. Many cities across Asia and the Pacific have, or are planning to create, integrated ticketing systems, for example, as part of 'mobility as a service' (MaaS) systems, where passengers can book tickets for their journeys across different modes of transport using a single application and payment channel (ESCAP, 2021). For example, in 2020, Beijing, China introduced the 'Mobility as a Service: Mobility for Green City' initiative, including a carbon credit-inclusive incentive scheme to encourage participation (Mobility Transition in China, 2021).

It is also important to enable easy interchange between different modes of transport. In Metro Manila, for example, the Parañaque Integrated Terminal Exchange is a multi-modal terminal with departure and arrival bays for buses, jeepneys and taxis. This facilitates the smooth transfer of passengers and reduces city centre congestion.

BOX 3-10   Real-time transport information systems for public transport in Greater Dhaka

Greater Dhaka, home to over 22 million people, is one of the world's most densely populated urban areas. Since 2005, as a result of a rising population and economic growth, GHG emissions from transport have been steadily increasing and are responsible for at least 15 per cent of CO_2 emissions from energy-related sectors. Greater Dhaka also suffers from severe traffic congestion, with an inefficient and inadequate public transport system.

The Government of Bangladesh aims to reduce its GHG emissions in the power, industry, and transport sectors by at least 5 per cent by 2030. To contribute to this, and make its operations more efficient, the Bangladesh Road Transport Company is digitalizing bus operations and management, with the support of the Climate Technology Centre and Network (CTCN) which facilitated a partnership with the Korea National University of Transportation.

The project has introduced a real-time bus information management system (BIMS). The system includes equipment on buses and at bus-stops for real-time tracking and monitoring, and software for data collection, server operation, data processing and analysis. The aim is to optimize public transportation and enable efficient operations for different stakeholders, such as bus drivers, passengers, bus operation companies and management authorities.

The project aims to increase the convenience of the public bus system so as to encourage people to use public rather than private transportation. It has been estimated that the BIMS could avoid up to 63,000 tons of carbon emissions annually.

Note: For more information, see, the CTCN case study at United Nations Environment Programme (UNEP), and UN Climate Technology Centre and Network (CTCN), "Development of framework for real-time transport information systems for public transport in Greater Dhaka", 2022. Available at https://www.ctc-n.org/technical-assistance/projects/development-framework-real-time-transport-information-systems-public

---

A number of Asia-Pacific countries are aiming to combine public transport and non-motorized options such as walking and cycling. These enable passengers to make more sustainable transport choices and reduce the use of private vehicles. Singapore has taken this concept further by envisioning '20-minute towns', where residents can access a range of services within 20 minutes in their neighbourhoods (UITP, 2021).

Improving fuel efficiency

While the transition to electric vehicles is underway it is also important to improve the fuel efficiency of motor vehicles. Countries in South-East Asia have adopted the ASEAN Fuel Economy Roadmap for the Transport Sector 2018–2025. This envisages transforming the subregion's light-duty vehicle market into one of the world's most fuel efficient. Between 2015 and 2025, it aims to reduce the average fuel consumption of new light-duty vehicles by 26 per cent (The ASEAN Secretariat, 2019).

3.4 Smart industry and trade

Production methods across Asia and the Pacific are being transformed by the Fourth Industrial Revolution, that integrates digital technologies into smart manufacturing processes which typically have lower carbon emissions. Digitalization is also enabling climate-smart trade, helping to reduce trade costs and make global supply chains more resilient.

Decarbonization in the steel industry

Steel is essential to most manufacturing and construction, and with population growth, industrial development, and urbanization the demand continues to grow, particularly in developing countries which are still undergoing industrial development and urbanization. However, every ton of steel production generates approximately 1.89 metric tons of CO_2.

Most of the world's leading steel companies have declared targets for carbon neutrality, but their current production methods still release significant emissions.[11, 12] Globally, the manufacture of 3 billion tons every year accounts for 20–25 per cent of all industrial emissions,[13] and 7–9 per cent of total emissions (World Steel Association, 2024).

The slow progress is partly due to the investment required and technological barriers. But there are new options on the horizon for low-carbon steel production based on technologies, such as reduction ironmaking (HyREX) which, instead of using coke as reduction agent, uses hydrogen (Figure 3-3). This technology can significantly reduce carbon emissions. Unlike in a blast furnace, where reduction and melting occur in a single furnace, in HyREX, the reduction and melting reactions occur in a fluidized bed reduction furnace and an electric furnace, respectively. In the Republic of Korea, the Ministry of Trade, Industry and Energy has supported the steel manufacturer POSCO in commercializing HyREX which is expected to contribute to about 40 per cent of the industrial sector's carbon reduction target.

FIGURE 3-3 **Evolution of steel production process**

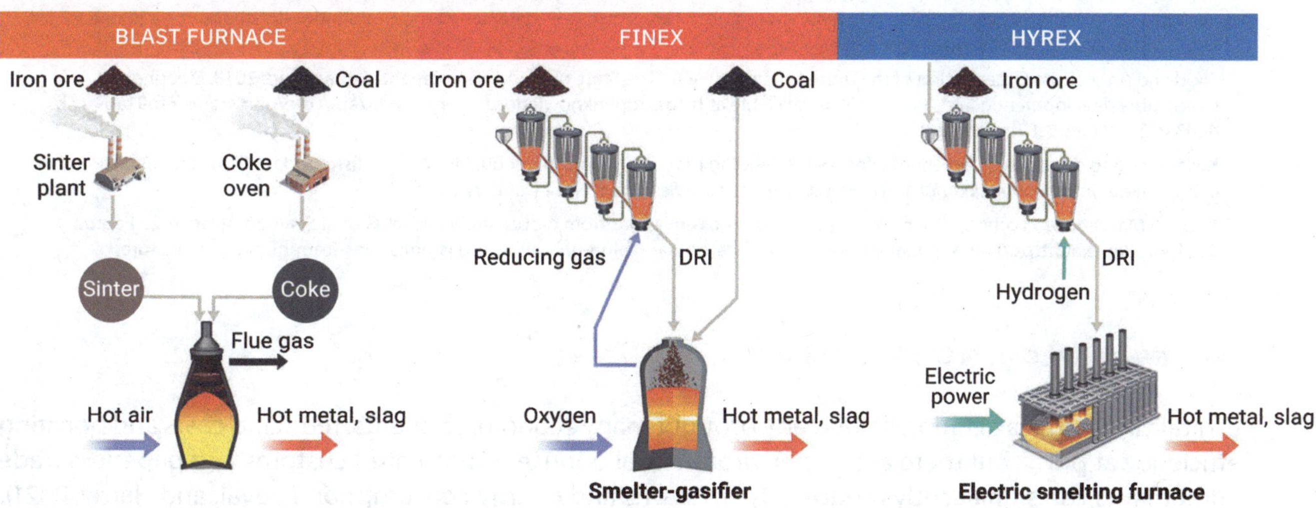

Source: POSCO, "Breakthrough hydrogen reduction ironmaking technology with near-zero emission", n.d. Available at https://www.posco.co.kr/homepage/docs/eng7/jsp/hyrex/

Note: The traditional blast furnace uses coke as a reducing agent. The more efficient FINEX process, introduced in the early 2000s, uses iron ore fines and non-coking coal. The latest, low-carbon HyREX process uses hydrogen as a reducing agent.

11 Carbon neutral: Zero net emissions of CO_2. Net zero: Zero net emissions of GHGs, including CO_2. Carbon neutral means balancing CO_2 emissions with carbon sinks.

12 ArcelorMittal: Net zero by 2050, and 35 per cent reduction by 2030; China's Baosteel: Net zero by 2050, and 30 per cent reduction by 2035; Nippon Steel: Net zero in 2050, and 30 per cent reduction by 2030; and POSCO, South Korea: Net zero by 2050, and 37 per cent reduction by 2030.

13 Energy sector 73.2 per cent (Industry energy 24 per cent, transport energy 16 per cent and building energy 18 per cent).

Smart industry and sustainable manufacturing

In the Asia-Pacific region, the industrial sector accounts for an estimated 24.5 per cent of carbon emissions by sector (IEA, n.d.). Many companies are investing in smart manufacturing with cleaner and more efficient technologies that can reduce their carbon footprints, by leveraging modular production systems, for example, using real-time monitoring and more efficient product customization (IEEE, 2024).

For example, Huawei Digital Power, a leading global provider of digital power products, is adopting renewable energy sources like solar and wind power. It is also implementing waste management systems that prioritize recycling and minimize waste generation.

BOX 3-11   Smart aquaculture in Indonesia

Globally the aquaculture industry contributes around 0.5 per cent of anthropogenic GHG emissions. Aquaculture is a relatively young industry with great scope for technical innovation. Fish feeding, for example can be improved with AI-powered smart feeders using real-time video images to fine-tune the quantity of feed dispensed, or when to stop feeding altogether if the fish are not hungry.

Indonesia has the world's second-largest aquaculture industry, and around 3.34 million fish farmers who rely on manual feeding methods. With over 30,000 farmers using the smart feeders from eFishery, however, the result was a 20 per cent increase in profit, a 45 per cent increase in incomes, and a reduction in nutrient runoff of over 30 per cent.

Indonesia's national Digital Roadmap supports projects, like eFishery, to contribute to the NDC which aims to reduce GHG emissions by 1,953 $MtCO_2e$ by 2030.

Sources:

Bonnie Waycott, "Can carbon mitigation strategies for aquafeeds help cut aquaculture's greenhouse gas emissions?" Global Seafood Alliance, 12 December 2022. Available at https://www.globalseafood.org/advocate/can-carbon-mitigation-strategies-for-aquafeeds-help-cut-aquacultures-greenhouse-gas-emissions/

Food and Agriculture Organization of the United Nations (FAO), "The State of World Fisheries and Aquaculture 2018: Meeting the sustainable development goals", (Rome, 2018). Available at https://openknowledge.fao.org/server/api/core/bitstreams/6fb91ab9-6cb2-4d43-8a34-a680f65e82bd/content

Kosemani, and others, "Assessment of effect of fish feeding practices on the water quality of some fishponds in Ekiti State Fish Farm, Ado Ekiti, Nigeria", *International Journal of Fisheries and Aquatic Studies*, vol. 5, No. 2 (January 2017).

Michael MacLeod, and others, "Quantifying greenhouse gas emissions from global aquaculture", Global Seafood Alliance, 22 February 2021. Available at https://www.globalseafood.org/advocate/quantifying-greenhouse-gas-emissions-from-global-aquaculture/

Climate-smart digital trade facilitation

Digitalizing trade facilitation has already brought many economic benefits, reducing costs and boosting efficiency at ports, but there are also environmental bonuses. Automated customs and paperless trade agreements can significantly reduce CO_2 emissions and energy consumption (Duval, and Hardy, 2021).

ESCAP has quantified the savings in GHG emissions if all trade-related paper documents in the Asia-Pacific region are ultimately replaced by digital documents and data exchange, as envisaged in the Framework Agreement on Facilitation of Cross-Border Paperless Trade in Asia and the Pacific. Even with conservative assumptions, the emissions saved by fully digitalizing a single end-to-end trade transaction are equivalent to those absorbed by 1.5 trees. For the Asia-Pacific region, this implies savings of about 13 million tons of CO_2 emissions annually, equivalent to the carbon captured by 400 million trees. Rather than through the direct savings of paper and ink however, the results are driven largely by efficiency gains from handling information digitally. Therefore, accession by all ESCAP members to the Framework Agreement would enable more countries to capture the environmental benefits from trade digitalization.

3.5 Digital data centres

Today's digital societies may appear to operate through an invisible cloud but ultimately are grounded in huge physical data centres; buildings with large numbers of servers that store and share data and applications. Data centres constitute the core of the digital society and economy, powering everything from everyday commerce, to cryptocurrencies, to all manner of government services.

Nevertheless, they themselves consume enormous amounts of energy. In 2022, data centres worldwide consumed 460 TWh, or 2 per cent of total electricity demand. By 2026, global electricity consumption of data centres, cryptocurrencies and AI is expected to range between 620 and 1050 TWh (IEA, 2024). By the end of 2026, there are likely to be 1,200 hyperscale data centres (Le Maistre, 2022).

An increasing amount of this computing power and energy is being devoted to AI. Sophisticated high-functioning generative AI systems, such as ChatGPT, consume huge quantities of data, and demand far more computer power than traditional search engines like Google. By 2027, Morgan Stanley has estimated that, for this and other purposes, generative AI will account for more than three-quarters of global data-centre power demand. The IEA expects that the power consumption for AI data centres will increase ten-fold from its 2022 level.

FIGURE 3-4　**Hyperscale data centre forecast**

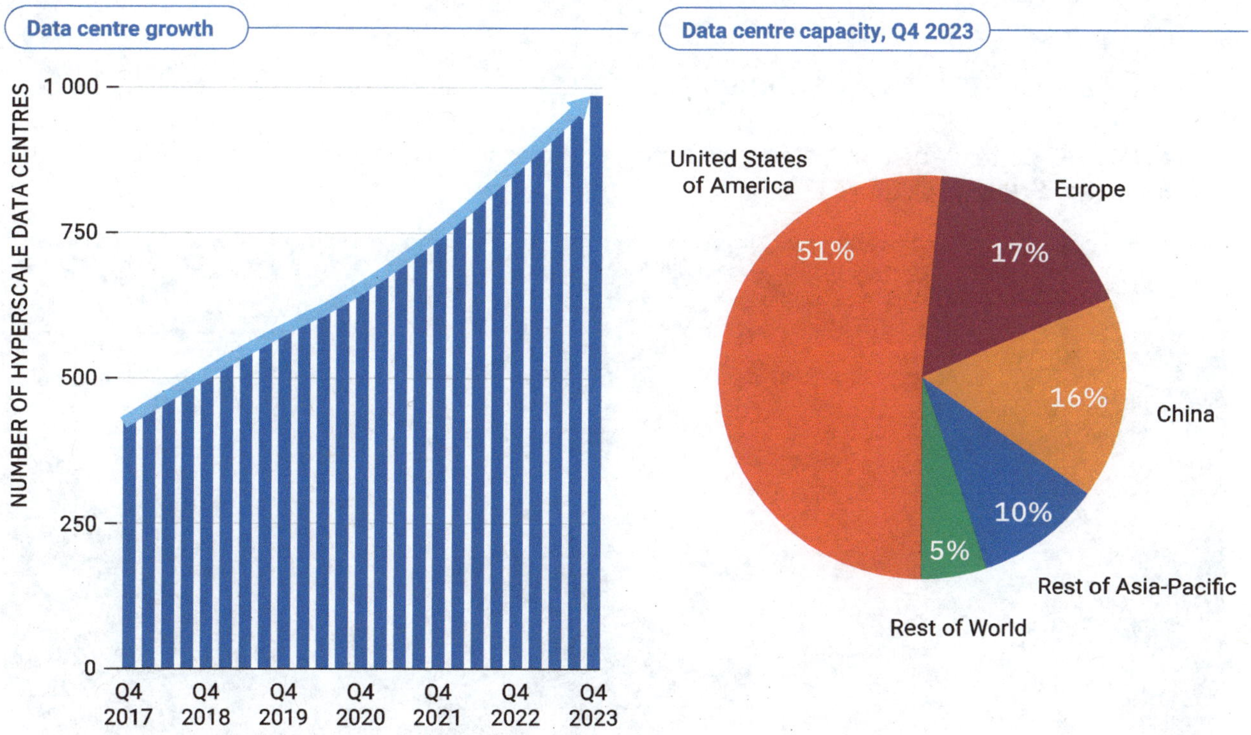

Source: Synergy Research Group, "Hyperscale data centers hit the thousand mark; total capacity is doubling every four years", 17 April 2024. Available at https://www.srgresearch.com/articles/hyperscale-data-centers-hit-the-thousand-mark-total-capacity-is-doubling-every-four-years

Keeping data centres cool

The operations of data centres can be optimized using intelligent energy management systems (Box 3-12) along with renewable energy such as solar (Box 3-13). These utilize AI and other smart systems, such as predictive analytics and intelligent power distribution units, to forecast demand, and adjust energy allocation dynamically through switching power, or moving and consolidating data workloads. While energy management systems are still a relatively new development, intelligent systems provide a clear pathway to achieving more efficient and greener data centre operations.

BOX 3-12   Optimizing data centre energy use

Intelligent energy management systems can be seamlessly applied to data centre operations.

Schneider Electric's EcoStruxure Power, for example, uses analytics and automation to optimize energy usage, enhance power distribution and improve overall operational efficiency. This is achieved through real-time monitoring and control, leading to a 20 per cent increase in energy savings and a reduction of carbon emissions.

Eaton's Intelligent Power Manager software, on the other hand, integrates with virtualized environments, which are commonly used in data centres to enable sophisticated monitoring, management and optimization of power usage across various data centres.

Source: Schneider Electric, "What is EcoStruxure Power?" 2024. Available at https://www.se.com/sg/en/work/campaign/innovation/ power-distribution.jsp

BOX 3-13   The United Nations Global Service Centre uses a sustainable data centre

The UNGSC Data Centre in Valencia, United Nations Information Communication Technology Facility (UNICTF)

Source: United Nations Global Service Centre (UNGSC).

The United Nations Global Service Centre (UNGSC) is the leading provider for the UN's digital technology and supply chain needs.

To boost sustainability, UNGSC has taken three overall measures:

Infrastructure Monitoring System: A software tool monitors the status and energy consumption in real time. This allows the centre to access historical data, employ AI to analyse and predict possible failures, identify peak consumption periods, and take pre-emptive measures to extend the life of infrastructure and reduce power consumption.

<table>
<tr><td>BOX 3-13</td><td>...continued</td></tr>
</table>

Infrastructure Efficiency: Since 2014, despite increasing capacity, overall power consumption has fallen by 10 per cent, through four efficiency measures: (1) keeping some of the uninterruptible power supplies in standby mode, with estimated annual savings of 350 MWh; (2) the use of polyvinyl chloride curtains to enhance the efficiency of air circulation; (3) a free cooling system which allows outside cold air to enter the centre when the external temperature is below 18°C; and (4) reducing electricity consumption in the condensers by evaporating water in a stream of warm, dry air.

Data Centre Building Power Consumption 2015–2024

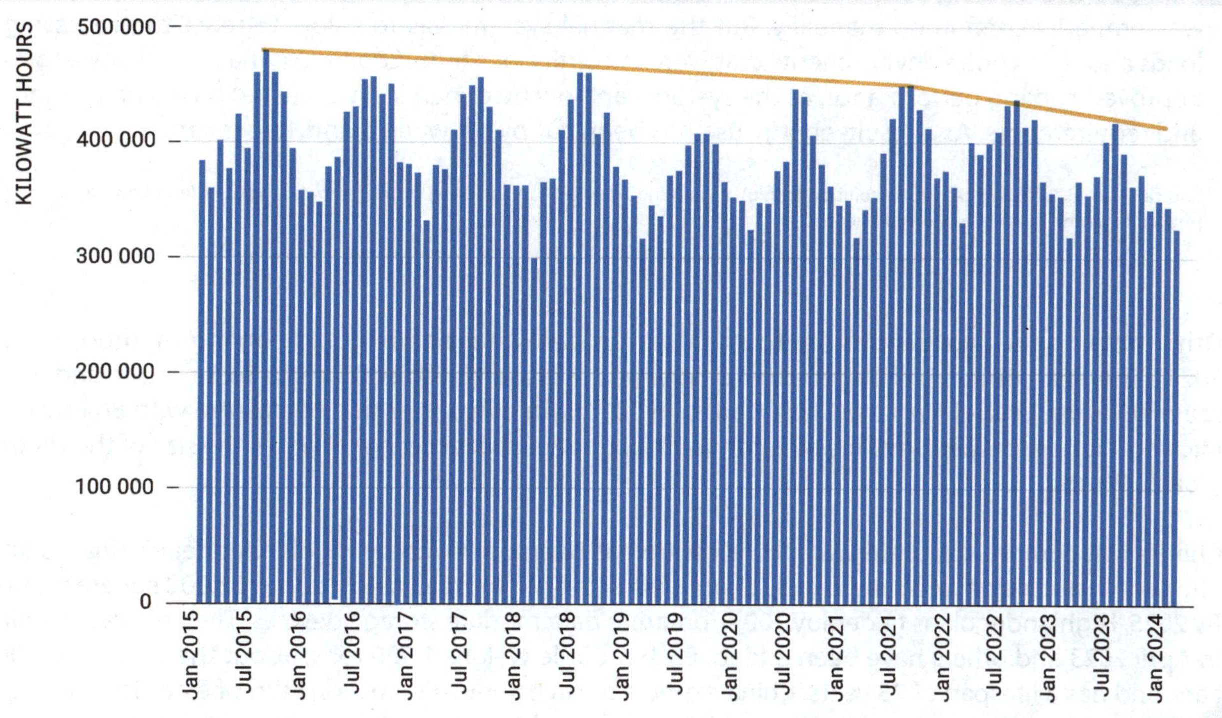

Source: United Nations Global Service Centre (UNGSC).

Note: Despite increasing capacity, overall power use has fallen.

Renewable energy: At the United Nations Information Communication Technology Facility in Valencia, all power which covers the data centre's electricity consumption is provided by a solar farm comprising 3,800 solar panels and 69 inverters, generating 850 kW of power. Since 2012, this has generated a total of 9,667,846 kWh resulting in savings of €1,700,000 and preventing the release of 1,334,163 kg of CO_2 into the atmosphere. There are also plans to install 3,000 additional solar panels along with a system to store excess energy generated during peak hours for use during the night.

UNGSC holds the following environmental and energy efficiency certifications: Uptime Certified Institute: *III Tier Facility*; International Organization for Standardization: *ISO 20000 – Service Management*; *ISO 14001 – Environmental Management*; CEEDA Gold Certification: *Energy Efficient Data Centre*; Information Security Management System: *ISO 27000 Certified*; European Code of Conduct for Data Centres: *Award Winner*

To learn more, visit ungsc.org.

One of the main tasks is cooling thousands of processors that typically run very hot, but this too can be optimized using AI (Box 3-14). Real-time information can be collected from sensors that measure ambient temperature and humidity. These data, along with information on server load, are fed into algorithms that can adjust cooling operations based on actual need rather than pre-determined schedules. This consumes less electricity while ensuring optimal environmental conditions, thus making data centres more sustainable and climate friendly.

BOX 3-14 Huawei's AI-powered cooling system for data centres

Huawei has used an AI-powered cooling optimization system called 'iCooling@AI' to improve the cooling of the Central Plains Data Centre in Henan, China. Previously, cooling was primarily configured manually. But the manual system was too slow to react to processing loads and data centre environments that were in continuous flux. iCooling@AI has saved power and improved cooling performance, as the system can now be dynamically adjusted based on changes and requirements. As a result, energy use has been cut by between 6 and 15 per cent.

Source: Huawei, "iCooling@AI: A cool solution for global warming", May 2021. Available at https://www.huawei.com/en/huaweitech/publication/winwin/40/henan-unicom-icooling

---

Other options for data centres are to site them under water or use liquid cooling methods (Barry, 2023). The first commercial underwater centre was Microsoft's Project Natick, 36.5 metres under the sea off Orkney, United Kingdom. This started in 2018 with a two-year trial of a centre with 864 servers. Microsoft is now preparing to install a commercial undersea data centre 12 times the size of the UK trial (Roach, 2020).

China's first commercial underwater data centre has been deployed by Highlander near Hainan Island. The centre, at a depth of 35 metres, is roughly the size of 13 football fields, about 68,000 square metres. By 2025, Highlander plans to deploy 100 submarine data module storage devices. The first was installed in April 2023 and others have been added. Each module weighs 1,300 tons, about the weight of 1,000 cars, and has a lifespan of 25 years. China expects to save about 122 million kWh of electricity annually with data centres located under water, which is comparable to the average electricity usage of 160,000 Chinese citizens (Judge, 2022).

3.6 Digital transformations for disaster risk reduction

Asia and the Pacific is the world's most disaster-prone region, but digital technologies are helping to reduce the risks and improve disaster management by cutting both human casualties and economic losses.

ESCAP's Risk and Resilience Portal, for example, is an innovative digital platform that can deepen policymakers' understanding of the disaster-climate-health nexus. The portal provides risk scenarios, calculating the economic costs, identifying multi-hazard risk hotspots, and also suggesting adaptation priorities for 56 countries. To support informed decision-making, the portal provides socioeconomic information and contextual analysis on a variety of hazards, risks and vulnerabilities.

Space technology applications, big data and generative analytics

Accurate and timely information on climate risks is now available from space technology applications involving satellite-generated data and geographic information systems. Increasingly this is being combined with generative AI applications and big data analytics to predict, monitor and mitigate climate risks and impacts so as to boost adaptive capacity (ADB, 2021).

Global Forest Watch Platform, for example, uses geospatial data to monitor and track deforestation in near-real-time and enable governments and organizations to take swift action (Lenox, 2021). The European Space Agency's Climate Change Initiative also uses geospatial data to monitor and track climate change indicators, such as sea-level rise, icesheet mass balance, and GHG concentrations (European Space Agency, n.d.).

These systems increasingly exploit AI to predict extreme weather events, such as hurricanes, floods, and droughts. AI tools are processing vast amounts of climate data, predicting future climate scenarios, implementing more energy-efficient measures, and improving the capacity to manage vulnerability. As illustrated in Figure 3-5, AI can be integrated throughout the processes, from data input to model development to operations.

FIGURE 3-5   **Simplified AI life cycle for disaster risk reduction**

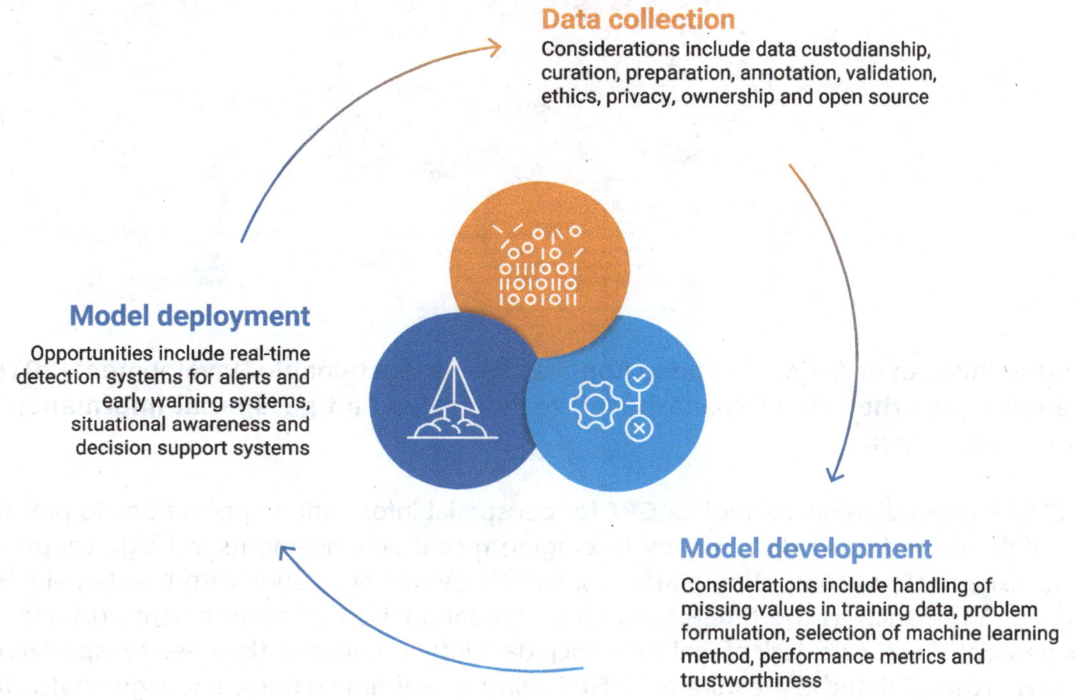

Source: Adapted from, Monique Kuglitsch, and others, "Artificial Intelligence for Disaster Risk Reduction: Opportunities, Challenges and Prospects", *World Meteorological Organization (WMO) Bulletin*, vol. 71, No. 1 (2022). Available at https://library.wmo.int/viewer/46824/download?file=WMO_Bulletin_71%281%29_en.pdf&type=pdf&navigator=1

In North and East Asia, for example, the substantial reductions in mortality and economic losses from typhoons, for instance, can be attributed to advanced numerical weather prediction and big data applications that have enabled impact-based forecasting and risk-informed early warning products. Further opportunities for flood forecasting can come from ensemble prediction systems. For predicting the location and severity of floods, such systems can also employ machine learning to find significant data patterns.

Leveraging AI and spatiotemporal data for SDG monitoring and assessment also enables governments to effectively allocate resources, identify populations at risk of being left behind, and adapt strategies to the evolving challenges, thereby promoting accountability and evidence-based decision-making. For example, local governments in Indonesia are extending the technology stack to the use of ethical AI, ensuring participatory modelling in the development of AI models, and supporting AI models to be trained in using sex- and age- disaggregated data. These are helping to map and access multiple indicators for SDGs 1, 2, 6, 11, 13, 15 and 17, while keeping vulnerable and marginalized populations in focus.

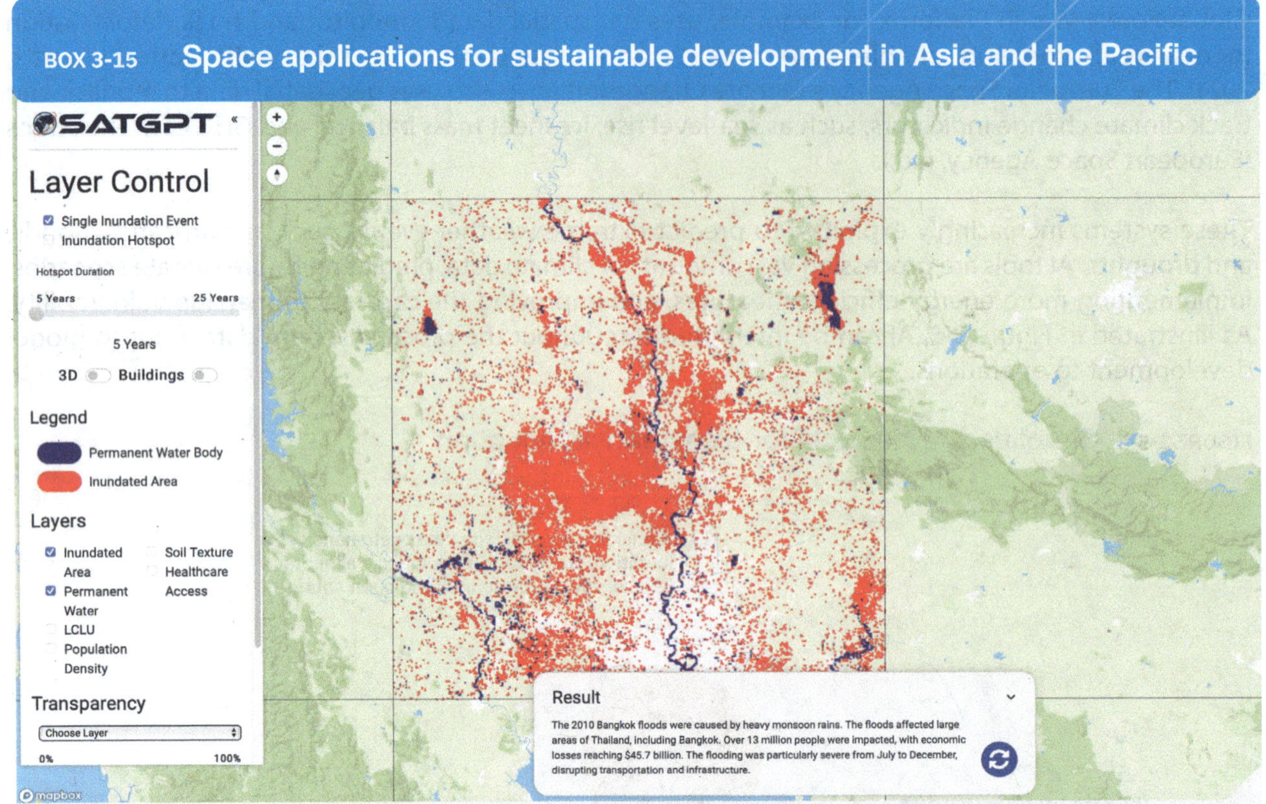

The Asia-Pacific Plan of Action on Space Applications for Sustainable Development (2018–2030)[a] emphasizes the role of space-based technologies and geospatial information in disaster risk reduction.

In 2024, ESCAP created an online tool SatGPT for geospatial information applications to plot the hotspots of floods and other disasters, by leveraging recent advancements in Large Language Models (LLMs) and cloud computing platforms. SatGPT overcomes issues with traditional flood mapping methods, such as the time-consuming manual analysis of remote sensing imagery, complex geospatial software, lack of real-time sociodata integration, and the need for specialized technical expertise. With the key feature of SatGPT being its real-time natural language service, the goal of SatGPT is to promote the availability, accessibility, affordability and actionability of remote sensing applications and geospatial data. This helps to provide a more sustainable and informed approach to managing the health of our planet.

In collaboration with the United Nations University (UNU), ESCAP developed operational tools using big Earth data, cloud computing and AI for disaster risk hotspot mapping to decrease the costs and time to identify disaster risk hotspots in the region. These tools were listed in the UN Climate Change Innovation Compendium and won innovation awards. ESCAP also collaborated with the UNU Institute for Water, Environment and Health in developing the online course "Introduction to Geospatial Data Analysis with ChatGPT and Google Earth Engine", which attracted over 2750 enrolments from over 33 countries in Asia and the Pacific.

a   United Nations University, "Introduction to Geospatial Data Analysis with ChatGPT and Google Earth Engine", n.d. Available at https://lc.unu.edu/courses/course-v1:UNU-INWEH+INWEH-20+2023_T4/about

Sources:

United Nations Economic and Social Commission for Asia and the Pacific (ESCAP), "Asia-Pacific plan of action on space applications for sustainable development (2018–2030)", Policy brief, 12 February 2019. Available at https://www.unescap.org/resources/asia-pacific-plan-action-space-applications-sustainable-development-2018–2030

United Nations Economic and Social Commission for Asia and the Pacific (ESCAP), "Jakarta Ministerial Declaration on Space Applications for Sustainable Development in Asia and the Pacific", 26 October 2022. ESCAP/MCSASD/2022/3/Add.1

United Nations University, "UNU-INWEH's World Flood Mapping Tool is one of 2021's '100 Greatest Innovations'", Press release, 30 November 2021. Available at https://unu.edu/press-release/unu-inwehs-world-flood-mapping-tool-one-2021s-100-greatest-innovations

BOX 3-16 A digital climate information system platform in Cambodia

Cambodia is highly susceptible to natural disasters and to the adverse effects of climate change which could reduce GDP growth by 6.6 per cent by 2030 and by 9.8 per cent by 2050, particularly affecting rural communities who depend heavily on natural resources.

Policymakers, planners, and practitioners at both national and sub-national levels have been hampered by the lack of climate-related information. To address this gap, the Climate Technology Centre and Network (CTCN) has supported the creation of a Local Climate Information System for Climate Change Adaptation (LISA). This user-friendly online platform allows stakeholders to explore future climate scenarios, comprehend potential impacts, and consider adaptation options. It is being piloted in Battabang municipality.

LISA integrates climate risk assessments and climate projections, empowering policymakers and planners with reliable data. This helps boost awareness of climate impacts and enables evidence-based decision-making and adaptation strategies.

Source: United Nations Environment Programme (UNEP), and UN Climate Technology Centre and Network (CTCN), "Climate risk assessment for subnational adaptation and establishment of a local climate information system for climate change adaptation (LISA) in Cambodia", 29 January 2021. Available at https://www.ctc-n.org/technical-assistance/projects/climate-risk-assessment-subnational-adaptation-and-establishment

BOX 3-17 Digital early warning systems for flooding in Bangkok

Bangkok is a sprawling low-lying coastal metropolis that faces escalating climate-related threats, including rising sea levels and more-frequent extreme weather phenomena. The economic costs of these threats could run into billions of dollars. Almost any part of Bangkok can flood, but the greatest impacts are felt by the urban populations, particularly those from disadvantaged groups.

To develop an urban flood early warning system for a high-risk catchment area, the Bangkok Metropolitan Administration sought technical assistance from the Climate Technology Centre and Network (CTCN). The CTCN responded with a system which provides essential information on flood risk zones to residents and commuters through a user-friendly web and mobile platform, thereby enhancing preparedness and response.

The CTCN has also facilitated training sessions on early warning management, equipping stakeholders with the necessary skills, and offered recommendations on expanding the early warning system citywide.

Note: for more information on Bangkok's Early Warning System, see United Nations Environment Programme (UNEP), and UN Climate Technology Centre and Network (CTCN), "Strengthening Bangkok's Early Warning System to respond to climate induced flooding", 29 January 2016. Available at https://www.ctc-n.org/technical-assistance/projects/strengthening-bangkok-s-early-warning-system-respond-climate-induced

Photo: Arisa Chattasa/Unsplash

BOX 3-18 **Satellites monitor air pollution in the Philippines**

The Pan-Asia Partnership for Geospatial Air Pollution information (PAPGAPi) project is being implemented by the Philippine Space Agency in partnership with organizations in eight other countries; Bangladesh, Cambodia, Indonesia, the Lao People's Democratic Republic, Mongolia, the Republic of Korea, Thailand, and Viet Nam. The project provides training and workshops to help staff make more use of high-resolution remote sensing data from sources, such as the Geostationary Environment Monitoring Spectrometer and the Pandora Spectrometer, for precise and in-depth study of air quality in pilot cities.

One such city is Metro Manila, which is close to the Taal volcano whose eruptions can pollute the air and damage health. In 2023, remote sensing data made available through PAPGAPi enabled a better understanding of the impact of the Taal eruption on the Metro Manila population. Implementing the PAPGAPi project is also helping to build capacity for regional and subregional dialogue for evidence-based policymaking on air pollution monitoring and management.

Note: For more information on the Pan-Asia Partnership for Geospatial Air Pollution information, see United Nations Economic and Social Commission for Asia and the Pacific (ESCAP),"Building the Pan Asia Partnership for Geospatial Air Pollution Information (PAPGAPI)", n.d. Available at https://www.unescap.org/projects/papgapi ; and Philippine Space Agency (PhilSA), "Pan-Asia Partnership for Geospatial Air Pollution Information Project and the Pandora Asia Network (PAPGAPI-PAN) Philippines Project", n.d. Available at https://philsa.gov.ph/papgapi-pan/

BOX 3-19 **Emergency Internet services in Tonga and Vanuatu**

For high-speed Internet connectivity, remote island communities in the Pacific have been supported by the private-sector company SpaceX, whose Starlink service can provide Internet access via around 1,600 low Earth orbit satellites.

In 2023, the twin tropical cyclones, Judy and Kevin, both of category-4 intensity, made landfall in Vanuatu, cutting mobile network coverage by approximately 50 per cent nationwide. To support emergency response efforts, Starlink loaned the Government ten satellite terminals. These were configured and activated in priority provincial emergency operations centres through the Emergency Telecommunications Cluster (ETC), a global network of organizations that provide shared communications services in humanitarian emergencies. The Pacific ETC also prepared a Starlink installation guide for technicians, and a user guide for the Vanuatu national clusters in English, French and Bislama.

Similarly in Tonga, following the eruption in 2022 of the Tonga-Hunga Ha'apai volcano, the country lost all Internet communications. Within 25 days, Starlink had provided broadband Internet services through an ad-hoc gateway station in Fiji and 50 very small aperture terminals (VSATs) provided free of charge by SpaceX.

Sources:

Radio New Zealand (RNZ), "Musk's Starlink may provide permanent internet solution for some Tongan islands", 9 February 2022. Available at https://www.rnz.co.nz/news/national/461162/musk-s-starlink-may-provide-permanent-internet-solution-for-some-tongan-islands

Kirsty Needham, "Musk's Starlink connects remote Tonga villages still cut off after tsunami", *Reuters*, 23 February 2023. Available at https://www.reuters.com/world/asia-pacific/musks-starlink-connects-remote-tonga-villages-still-cut-off-after-tsunami-2022-02-23/#:~:text=SYDNEY%2C%20Feb%2023%20(Reuters),eruption%20and%20tsunami%20in%20January

BOX 3-20   Monitoring air pollution in Thailand and the lower Mekong region

During the dry season in South-East Asia, the combination of arid vegetation and small-scale human-induced fires often leads to forest fires. These create a polluting haze that floats across the subregion dispersing components, such as sulphates, nitrates, ammonia, sodium chloride, black carbon, mineral dust and water.

The Rajamangala University of Technology in Thailand, through partnerships with USAID and NASA, has developed a pollution monitoring system, the SERVIR-Mekong Air Quality Explorer. The system covers Thailand and the lower Mekong region, which includes the Lao People's Democratic Republic, Cambodia and southern parts of Viet Nam.[a]

The tool utilizes geospatial data from satellite sensors to provide data for historical and near real-time visualizations of air quality and fire hotspots and enable officials to formulate interventions to put out the fires. It also offers air-quality forecasts that can be accessed and visualized using machine-learning algorithms from NASA's GEOS global forecast model.[b]

Coverage of the SERVIR-Mekong Air Quality Explorer

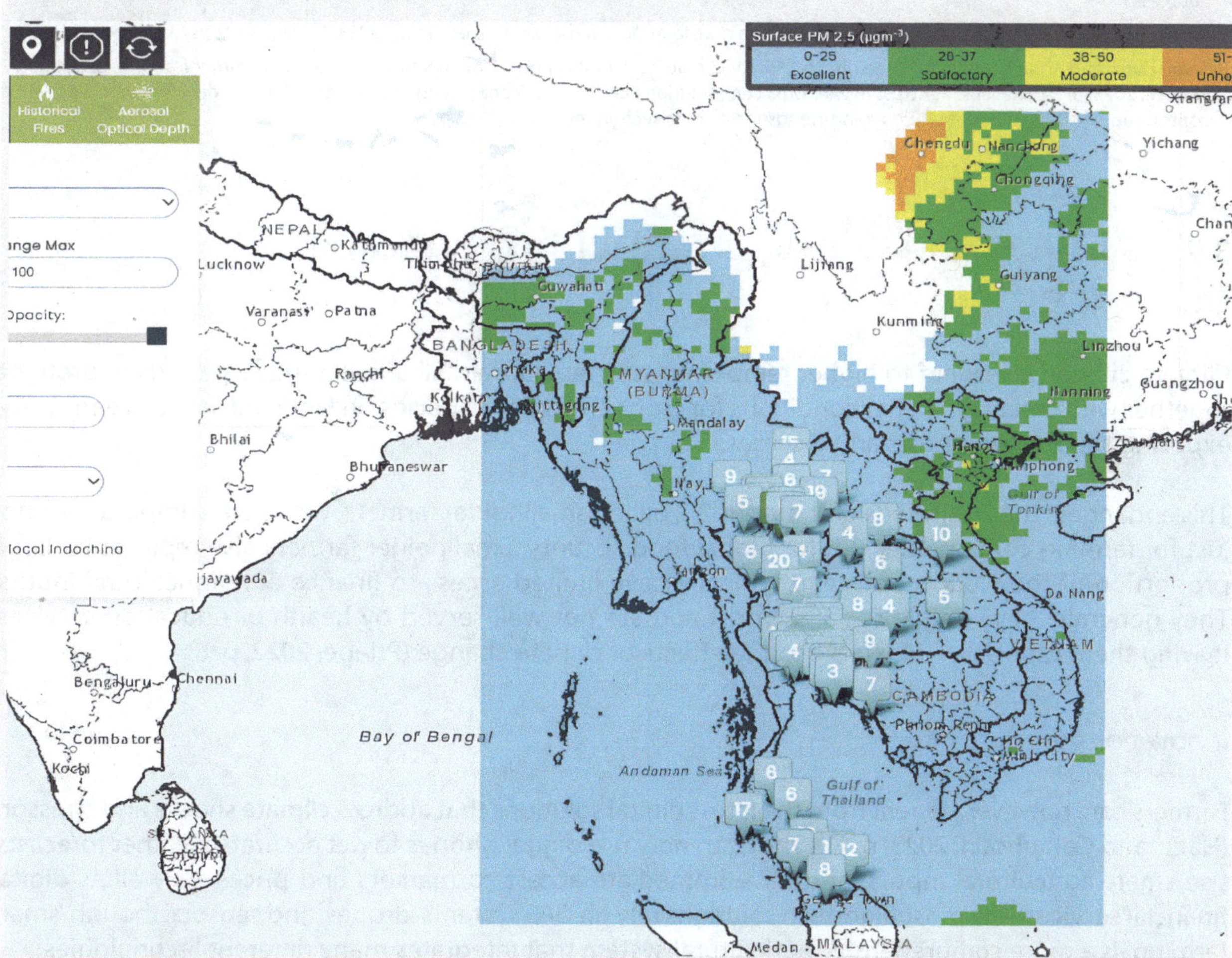

Source: Asian Disaster Preparedness Center (ADPC), "Mekong Air Quality Explorer: Enabling a sustainable landscape-scale agricultural management through fire and air quality monitoring", 2022. Available at https://aqatmekong-servir.adpc.net/en/home/

Note: The Mekong Air Quality Explorer can capture various datapoints regarding air quality in the blue-shaded area of the map.

a SERVIR, "SERVIR-Mekong's Geospatial Technology Helps Combat Forest Fires in Northern Thailand", 11 August 2021. Available at https://servirglobal.net/news/servir-mekongs-geospatial-technology-helps-combat-forest-fires-northern-thailand

b Ibid.

BOX 3-21 **Unlocking the power of climate data and analytics in the Philippines**

The Philippines has one of the world's longest coastlines and a rich biodiversity ecosystem. It is also one of the countries most affected by extreme weather events, suffering from an average of 20 cyclones per year along with regular floods and droughts, and occasional earthquakes and volcanic eruptions.

In the aftermath of Typhoon Haiyan, the founder of the private sector enterprise, Komunidad, resolved to develop effective strategies for businesses to enhance their resilience in the face of natural disasters. He manually compiled comprehensive reports and disseminated them as email alerts. This initiative laid the foundation for Komunidad, which was officially established in June 2021.

Today, Komunidad is a digital platform which helps governments across Asia and the Pacific to monitor, plan and prepare for weather events more efficiently and accurately and enables vulnerable communities to respond to disasters. Komunidad provides data and analytics software-as-a-service and generates SMS alerts and data summaries for local governments to enable them to respond, mobilize resources and evacuate communities.

Sources:

Komunidad Global Pte Ltd., "Accelerating the transition to a climate-resilient and low carbon economy", 2023. Available at https://komunidad.global/

Samir Hafiz, and Anna Colquhoun, "Emerging trends for climate tech innovations", Global System for Mobile Communications Association (GSMA), 2023, p. 29. Available at https://www.gsma.com/solutions-and-impact/connectivity-for-good/mobile-for-development/wp-content/uploads/2023/06/GSMA_Emerging-trends-for-climate-tech-innovations_2023.pdf

3.7 Climate resilience for agriculture and biodiversity ecosystems

Climate change is leading to higher temperatures, irregular rainfall and extended periods of drought, together with creating harsher conditions for crops and animal species on land and in the oceans while exposing them to new pests and diseases.

This endangers the livelihoods of the world's 2 billion smallholder farmers, with severe implications not just for farming communities but for global food security. Smallholder farmers also represent a large proportion of the world's poor and typically have limited access to finance and agricultural inputs. They generally have fragile social support and are not well served by health or education services, leaving them especially vulnerable to the effects of climate change (Priebe, 2022, p. 8).

Innovations for agriculture

Farmers can, however, benefit from the latest digital solutions that address climate shocks and stressors (Hafiz, and Colquhoun, 2023, p. 11). They can now use digital phones to get accurate weather forecasts, use smart agricultural inputs, and have immediate access to markets and prices, as well as digital financial services. The most high-tech solutions rely on GPS systems, drones, and sensors, though 'smart farming' is a more comprehensive agricultural system that integrates many different technologies.

In the past, smallholder farmers have generally operated outside traditional banking systems. Now using only a smartphone they can log into fintech services, such as credit, insurance, remittances and government transfers without the need for a traditional bank account. Digital solutions, such as mobile money, can help smallholder farmers build resilience to climate change, including through affordable insurance against extreme weather events that uses automated processes, which eliminates the need for a claims assessor and thus speeds up payouts (Mulwa, 2023, p. 23).

BOX 3-22   A digital hub for farmers in Pakistan

Pakistan ranks eight out of 191 countries in vulnerability to climate change and has around 8.2 million smallholder farmers who face difficulties accessing high-quality data and weather information, with significant repercussions on food security.

BaKhabar Kissan is a digital hub providing farmers with a variety of services along the agricultural value chain. The services are accessible through a mobile app and interactive voice response, and include agricultural expertise, farming methods and hyperlocal weather information from their network of weather stations.

Sources:

BaKhabar Kissan (BKK), "Pakistan's leading agritech", 2023. Available at https://bkk.ag/

Samir Hafiz, and Anna Colquhoun, "Emerging trends for climate tech innovations", Global System for Mobile Communications Association (GSMA), 2023. Available at https://www.gsma.com/solutions-and-impact/connectivity-for-good/mobile-for-development/wp-content/uploads/2023/06/GSMA_Emerging-trends-for-climate-tech-innovations_2023.pdf

BOX 3-23   Credit profiles for dairy farmers in Nepal

To produce livestock feed, smallholder dairy farmers in Nepal depend on stable rainfall. Due to climate change, however, erratic rainfall patterns are reducing crops of livestock forage and leading to lower milk production. In addition, farmers find it difficult to borrow to tide them over lean spells or invest in agricultural inputs since they cannot establish credit profiles that would open up access to finance.

Farmers now can make use of Aloi, a digital platform for monitoring and tracking loan expenditure and repayments, which focuses on informal sector entrepreneurs. In collaboration with the Central Dairy Cooperative Association of Nepal, Aloi enables smallholder dairy farmers to offer their credit profiles for accessing loans. Aloi also offers training on topics such as agroforestry for fodder production.

Aloi works through verified merchants and deposit points. Like an automatic audit, it tracks financing flows using simple phones and without mobile Internet.

Source: Aloi Global, "Powering microfinance for informal sector business", 2024. Available at https://aloi.global/

Photo: Aloi Global

BOX 3-24   **Solar powered shrimp farming in the Philippines**

Shrimp farms require 24/7 electrically powered aeration to offer the shrimp sufficient oxygen to grow and thrive. Production is thus highly energy intensive. Much or all of this energy can come from solar installations.

The solar shrimp farm run by the San Andres Aquaculture Corporation (Sanacor), in the Philippines, is powered by a massive, ground-mounted 704kW solar photovoltaic system. This project is a collaboration between Huawei and local partners and allows Sanacor to maintain its operations while reducing the environmental impact. By tapping into renewable energy sources, Sanacor can reduce its reliance on traditional energy sources and contribute to a more sustainable aquaculture industry, while also contributing to the local economy.

Source: Manila Bulletin, "Solar power cuts Sanacor's operational costs", 29 November 2023. Available at https://mb.com.ph/2023/11/29/solar-power-cuts-sanacor-s-operational-costs

Climate technologies for natural resource management

An estimated 40 per cent of the world's extreme poor, around 250 million people, live in rural areas (Sharma, 2021, p. 21). They include many indigenous communities who often live in forested or savannah areas and rely on natural products, goods and services for shelter, livelihoods, food, water and energy security. Historically, they have been the custodians of much of the world's natural resources, but find themselves under increasing threats because of deforestation, the extension of agriculture and the encroachment of urban areas.

The marginalization of the rural poor reflects inequalities in the distribution of power and resources, and hence requires social and political solutions. However, some of the impacts can be reduced by better resource management and by using digital tools (Colquhoun, and others, 2023). For example, the use of big data is helping to predict air pollution and restore mangroves, while geospatial technologies are helping to map out water and soil resources.

To avoid deepening inequalities, indigenous peoples and other communities need to be involved in the choices and implementation of all activities that affect their lives. Often the better options are low-tech solutions especially when these can be co-created with the community. But, it is also important to understand the barriers that can limit their access to useful digital opportunities (Colquhoun, and others, 2023).

BOX 3-25   **The Monsoon Tea Company in Thailand**

Over the period 1973–2020, northern Thailand lost around one-fifth of its forests due to logging and the extension of agriculture, which threatened local communities and the area's biodiversity ecosystems.

Rather than cutting down trees to clear land, the Monsoon Tea Company grows tea in the forests, helping to improve biodiversity and prevent deforestation while providing local communities with stable sources of income.

The company is also developing a mobile app to empower farmers by making tea products traceable from end to end. The app will be used to collect data on biodiversity, combining AI-powered biosensors with traditional indicators. This can then be converted into a biodiversity scoring system that allows farmers to be rewarded with virtual biodiversity tokens.

Australia's Great Barrier Reef is endangered by climate-related coral bleaching. Scientists have now turned to AI to map and analyse the health of the reef and identify coral species. Machine learning algorithms can log species, predict extinction probabilities and assess global fisheries data. Automated analysis of uploaded images and information enables officials to map species distribution, assess richness levels and create biodiversity checklists by location.

This approach not only accelerates coral restoration, but also makes the reef ecosystem more resilient to future climate impacts. AI technology is also being used to address the issue of biosecurity by quickly detecting underwater pests and protecting native animals and plants.

Sources:

Great Barrier Reef Foundation, "Drones, AI and e-DNA keeping tabs on Great Barrier Reef and animal health", media release, 13 September 2022. Available at https://www.barrierreef.org/news/media-release/drones-ai-and-edna-keeping-tabs-on-great-barrier-reef-and-animal-health

José Anchieta C.C. Nunes, and others, "Speeding up coral reef conservation with AI-aided automated image analysis", *Nature Machine Intelligence*, vol. 2, No. 292 (June 2020).

Photo: Manny Moreno/Unsplash

Chapter 3 References

Acero, Juan A., and Ander Zozaya (n.d.). Cooling Singapore: Digital Urban Climate Twin (DUCT). Available at https://www.thegpsc.org/sites/gpsc/files/cooling_singapore_-_digital_urban_climate_twin.pdf

Aloi Global (2024). Powering microfinance for informal sector business. Available at https://aloi.global/#:~:text=Aloi%20is%20a%20software%20platform,Aloi

APN News (2021). SK ecoplant Develops eco-friendly AI-powered incinerator solution using AWS. 13 July. Available at https://www.apnnews.com/sk-ecoplant-develops-eco-friendly-ai-powered-incinerator-solution-using-aws/

Argyroudis, Sotirios, A., and others (2022). Digital technologies can enhance climate resilience of critical infrastructure. Climate Risk Management, vol. 35. Available at https://www.sciencedirect.com/science/article/pii/S2212096321001169

Asian Development Bank (ADB) (2021). *Digital technologies for climate action, disaster resilience, and environmental sustainability*. Philippines. Available at https://www.adb.org/sites/default/files/publication/700396/digital-technologies-climate-action.pdf

Asian Disaster Preparedness Center (ADPC) (2022). Mekong Air Quality Explorer: Enabling a sustainable landscape-scale agricultural management through fire and air quality monitoring. Available at https://aqatmekong-servir.adpc.net/en/home/

BaKhabar Kissan (BKK) (2023). Pakistan's leading agritech. Available at https://bkk.ag/

Barry, Holland (2023). AI, liquid cooling and the data center of the future. *Forbes*. 11 September. Available at https://www.forbes.com/sites/forbestechcouncil/2023/09/11/ai-liquid-cooling-and-the-data-center-of-the-future/?sh=6b81f6c3298d

Chorbog, Karim (2015). South Korea: Cutting Back on Food Waste. Pulitzer Center. 12 November. Available at https://pulitzercenter.org/stories/south-korea-cutting-back-food-waste

Colquhoun, Anna and others (2023). Exploring Barriers and Incentives to Digital Solutions in Natural Resource Management Global System for Mobile Communications Association (GSMA). March. Available at https://www.gsma.com/solutions-and-impact/connectivity-for-good/mobile-for-development/wp-content/uploads/2023/04/GSMA_Exploring-barriers-and-incentives-to-digital-solutions-in-Natural-Resource-Management_ClimateTech_2023.pdf

Destination Earth (n.d.). Available at https://destination-earth.eu

Duval, Yann, and Simon Hardy (2021). A primer on quantifying the environmental benefits of cross-border paperless trade facilitation. United Nations Economic and Social Commission of Asia and the Pacific (ESCAP), Trade, Investment and Innovation Division, Working Paper Series. 28 May. Available at https://www.unescap.org/kp/2021/primer-quantifying-environmental-benefits-cross-border-paperless-trade-facilitation

European Space Agency (n.d.). Climate Change Initiative. Available at https://climate.esa.int/en/about-us-new/climate-change-initiative/

Food and Agriculture Organization of the United Nations (FAO) (2018). *The State of World Fisheries and Aquaculture 2018: Meeting the sustainable development goals*. Rome. Available at https://openknowledge.fao.org/server/api/core/bitstreams/6fb91ab9-6cb2-4d43-8a34-a680f65e82bd/content

Food and Life Companies (2023). Sustainability Report 2023. 22 December. Available at https://www.food-and-life.co.jp/wp-content/uploads/pdf/sustainability/report2023.pdf

__________ (n.d.). Challenge to reduce food loss with DX. Available at https://food-and-life.co.jp/en/sustainability/sushisystem/

Frearson, Amy (2021). Digital twins are "big driver" towards net-zero cities say experts. Dezeen. 7 September. Available at https://www.dezeen.com/2021/09/07/digital-twins-climate-change-net-zero-cities/

Fu, H., Y. Shi, and Y. Zeng (2021). Estimating Smart Grid's Carbon Emission Reduction Potential in China's Manufacturing Industry Based on Decomposition Analysis. *Frontiers in Energy Research*, vol. 9 (June). Available at https://doi.org/10.3389/fenrg.2021.681244

Furness, Dyllan (2016). South Korea's smart garbage cans know how much waste you toss and charge accordingly. Digital Trends. 10 May. Available at https://www.digitaltrends.com/home/south-korea-waste/

Gent, Edd (2021). Can Earth's Digital Twins Help Us Navigate the Climate Crisis? IEEE Spectrum. 22 November. Available at https://spectrum.ieee.org/climate-models

George, Manju, Karen O'Regan, and Alexander Holst (2022). Digital solutions can reduce global emissions by up to 20%. Here's how. World Economic Forum. 23 May. Available at https://www.weforum.org/agenda/2022/05/how-digital-solutions-can-reduce-global-emissions/

Geospatial.SG (n.d.). Virtual Singapore. Available at https://www.sla.gov.sg/geospatial/gw/virtual-singapore

Global System for Mobile Communications Association (GSMA) (2024) *Making Circularity Work: How digital innovation enables circular economy approaches in waste management*. Available at https://www.gsma.com/solutions-and-impact/connectivity-for-good/mobile-for-development/gsma_resources/making-circularity-work-how-digital-innovation-enables-circular-economy-approaches-in-waste-management/

GovInsider (2024). Secure, seamless, and inclusive: How governments can accelerate digital IDs adoption. 8 January. Available at https://govinsider.asia/intl-en/article/secure-seamless-and-inclusive-how-governments-can-accelerate-digital-ids-adoption

Great Barrier Reef Foundation (2022). Drones, AI and e-DNA keeping tabs on Great Barrier Reef and animal health. Media release. 13 September. Available at https://www.barrierreef.org/news/media-release/drones-ai-and-edna-keeping-tabs-on-great-barrier-reef-and-animal-health

Hafiz, Samir, and Anna Colquhoun (2023). Emerging trends for climate tech innovations. Global System for Mobile Communications Association (GSMA). Available at https://www.gsma.com/solutions-and-impact/connectivity-for-good/mobile-for-development/wp-content/uploads/2023/06/GSMA_Emerging-trends-for-climate-tech-innovations_2023.pdf

Huawei (2021). iCooling@AI: A cool solution for global warming. May. Available at https://www.huawei.com/en/huaweitech/publication/winwin/40/henan-unicom-icooling

IBM (n.d.). What is a digital twin? Available at https://www.ibm.com/topics/what-is-a-digital-twin

International Energy Agency (IEA) (2018). Digitalization & Energy. Webinar. 7 February. Available at https://iea.blob.core.windows.net/assets/e5ffa993-ef78-49f7-8cfa-5375a41d074e/ieadigitalizationandenergywebinar-180220161419.pdf

__________ (2024). *Electricity 2024*. Paris. Available at https://www.iea.org/reports/electricity-2024

__________ (n.d.a). *Efficient Grid-Interactive Buildings: Future of buildings in ASEAN*. Available at https://iea.blob.core.windows.net/assets/71d1b69d-e8aa-49e5-9e0c-12c13d5a3a1f/EfficientGrid-InteractiveBuildings.pdf

__________ (n.d.b). Total CO_2 emissions. Available at https://www.iea.org/regions/asia-pacific/emissions

__________ (n.d.c). Unlocking the potential of distributed energy resources: Power system opportunities and best practices. Available at https://iea.blob.core.windows.net/assets/3520710c-c828-4001-911c-ae78b645ce67/UnlockingthePotentialofDERs_Powersystemopportunitiesandbestpractices.pdf

Institute of Electrical and Electronics Engineers (IEEE) (2024). Digital Technologies are the backbone of an energy-efficient industry 4.0. Available at https://climate-change.ieee.org/news/industry-4-0/

Jean, Koh (2023). Korea's new innovation strategy: Digital Platform Government. World Economic Forum. 13 January. Available at https://www.weforum.org/agenda/2023/01/davos23-korea-digital-platform-government/

Judge, Peter (2022). China's Highlander signs up to build commercial underwater data center on Hainan Island. Data Center Dynamics (DCD). 11 January. Available at https://www.datacenterdynamics.com/en/news/chinas-highlander-signs-up-to-build-commercial-underwater-data-center-on-hainan-island/

Kaye, Leon (2012). Swipe card technology introduced for food waste bins. *The Guardian*, 26 January. Available at https://www.theguardian.com/sustainable-business/south-korea-swipe-card-food-waste

KOMSCO (2019. Mobile ID (K-DID). Available at https://www.komsco.com/eng/contents/166

Komunidad Global Pte Ltd (2023). Accelerating the transition to a climate-resilient and low carbon economy. Available at https://komunidad.global/

Korea Environment Corporation (2023). RFID-based food wastes management system. Available at https://www.keco.or.kr/en/lay1/S295T387C404/contents.do

Kosemani, and others (2017). Assessment of effect of fish feeding practices on the water quality of some fishponds in Ekiti State Fish Farm, Ado Ekiti, Nigeria. *International Journal of Fisheries and Aquatic Studies*, vol. 5, No. 2 (January).

Kuglitsch, Monique, and others (2022). Artificial Intelligence for Disaster Risk Reduction: Opportunities, Challenges and Prospects. *World Meteorological Organization (WMO) Bulletin*, vol. 71, No. 1. Available at https://library.wmo.int/viewer/46824/download?file=WMO_Bulletin_71%281%29_en.pdf&type=pdf&navigator=1

Le Maistre, Ray (2022). How many hyperscale data centres does the world need? Hundreds more, it seems. *Telecom TV*. 24 March. Available at https://www.telecomtv.com/content/digital-platforms-services/how-many-hyperscale-data-centres-does-the-world-need-hundreds-more-it-seems-44015/

Lenox, Kelly (2021). Geospatial technology for environmental health research, decisions. Environmental Factor, National Institute of Environment Health Sciences. May. Available at https://factor.niehs.nih.gov/2021/5/science-highlights/geospatial

MacLeod, Michael, and others (2021). Quantifying greenhouse gas emissions from global aquaculture. Global Seafood Alliance. 22 February. Available at https://www.globalseafood.org/advocate/quantifying-greenhouse-gas-emissions-from-global-aquaculture/

Manila Bulletin (2023). Solar power cuts Sanacor's operational costs. 29 November. Available at https://mb.com.ph/2023/11/29/solar-power-cuts-sanacor-s-operational-costs

Mobility Transition in China (2021). Beijing MaaS Platform Launches "MaaS Mobility for Green City" Initiative. 26 May. Available at https://transition-china.org/mobilityposts/beijing-maas-platform-launches-maas-mobility-for-green-city-initiative/

Moore, Andrew (2023). Forest Biomaterials: AI-powered waste management system to revolutionize recycling. NC State University. 9 November. Available at https://cnr.ncsu.edu/fb/news/2023/11/ai-waste-management-recycling/

Mulwa, Judith (2023) Digitally Enabled Climate Finance: Access and delivery through mobile and digital technologies in low- and middle-income countries. Global System for Mobile Communications Association (GSMA). Available at https://www.gsma.com/solutions-and-impact/connectivity-for-good/mobile-for-development/wp-content/uploads/2023/04/GSMA-ClimateTech-Digitally-Enabled-Climate-Finance.pdf

National University of Singapore (2024). Cooling Singapore 2.0 – Digital Urban Climate Twin. 8 January. Available at https://fass.nus.edu.sg/srn/2024/01/08/cooling-singapore-2-0-digital-urban-climate-twin/

Needham, Kirsty (2023). Musk's Starlink connects remote Tonga villages still cut off after tsunami. *Reuters*, 23 February. Available at https://www.reuters.com/world/asia-pacific/musks-starlink-connects-remote-tonga-villages-still-cut-off-after-tsunami-2022-02-23/#:~:text=SYDNEY%2C%20Feb%2023%20(Reuters),eruption%20and%20tsunami%20in%20January

Nunes, José Anchieta C.C., and others (2020). Speeding up coral reef conservation with AI-aided automated image analysis. *Nature Machine Intelligence*, vol. 2, No. 292 (June).

Philippine Space Agency (PhilSA) (n.d.). Pan-Asia Partnership for Geospatial Air Pollution Information Project and the Pandora Asia Network (PAPGAPI-PAN) Philippines Project. Available at https://philsa.gov.ph/papgapi-pan/

POSCO (n.d.). Breakthrough hydrogen reduction ironmaking technology with near-zero emission. Available at https://www.posco.co.kr/homepage/docs/eng7/jsp/hyrex/

President Commission on Carbon Neutrality and Green Growth (n.d.). 2050 Carbon Neutrality of the Republic of Korea. Available at https://www.2050cnc.go.kr/eng/main/view

Priebe, Jan (2022). Data-driven advisory services for climate-smart smallholder agriculture. Global System for Mobile Communications Association (GSMA). September. Available at https://www.gsma.com/solutions-and-impact/connectivity-for-good/mobile-for-development/wp-content/uploads/2022/09/Data-driven-advisory-services-for-climate-smart-smallholder-agriculture.pdf

Radio New Zealand (RNZ) (2022). Musk's Starlink may provide permanent internet solution for some Tongan islands. 9 February. Available at https://www.rnz.co.nz/news/national/461162/musk-s-starlink-may-provide-permanent-internet-solution-for-some-tongan-islands

RFID World (2024). South Korea: Wastage of food reduced using RFID. 12 July. Available at https://rfidworld.ca/south-korea-wastage-of-food-reduced-using-rfid/887#:~:text=SK%20Telecom%2C%20with%20headquarters%20in%20South%20Korea%20has,a%20result%20of%20a%20reader%20attached%20to%20it.

Roach, John (2020). Microsoft finds underwater datacenters are reliable, practical and use energy sustainably. Microsoft. 4 September. Available at https://news.microsoft.com/source/features/sustainability/project-natick-underwater-datacenter/

Sáiz, Beatriz Sanz (2022). Metaverse: Could creating a virtual world build a more sustainable one? Ernest and Young Global Limited. Available at https://www.ey.com/en_gl/digital/metaverse-could-creating-a-virtual-world-build-a-more-sustainable-one

Schneider Electric (2024). What is EcoStruxure Power? Available at https://www.se.com/sg/en/work/campaign/innovation/power-distribution.jsp

Seoul Metropolitan Government (2016). Travel safely around the city even at night with Seoul's "Owl Bus". 22 December. Available at https://english.seoul.go.kr/travel-safely-around-city-even-night-seouls-owl-bus/

SERVIR (2021). SERVIR-Mekong's Geospatial Technology Helps Combat Forest Fires in Northern Thailand. 11 August. Available at https://servirglobal.net/news/servir-mekongs-geospatial-technology-helps-combat-forest-fires-northern-thailand

Sharma, Akanksha (2021) The Role of Digital and Mobile Enabled Solutions in Addressing Climate Change. Global System for Mobile Communications Association (GSMA). February. Available at https://www.gsma.com/solutions-and-impact/connectivity-for-good/mobile-for-development/wp-content/uploads/2021/03/The-Role-of-Digital-and-Mobile-Enabled-Solutions-in-Addressing-Climate-Change-Final..pdf

Sköld, Nannie (2021). UNHCR strengthens efforts on digital identity for refugees with Estonian support. United Nations High Commissioner for Refugees (UNHCR). 6 December. Available at https://www.unhcr.org/neu/70493-unhcr-strengthens-efforts-on-digital-identity-for-refugees-with-estonian-support.html

Synergy Research Group (2024). Hyperscale data centers hit the thousand mark; total capacity is doubling every four years. 17 April. Available at https://www.srgresearch.com/articles/hyperscale-data-centers-hit-the-thousand-mark-total-capacity-is-doubling-every-four-years

The ASEAN Secretariat (2019). ASEAN Fuel Economy Roadmap for the Transport Sector 2018-2025: With Focus on Light-Duty Vehicles. Jakarta. Available at https://asean.org/wp-content/uploads/2021/08/ASEAN-Fuel-Economy-Roadmap-FINAL-2.pdf

The Government of the Republic of Korea (2020). 2050 Carbon Neutral Strategy of the Republic of Korea: Towards a sustainable and green society. December. Available at https://unfccc.int/sites/default/files/resource/LTS1_RKorea.pdf

Union Internatonale des Transports Publics (UITP) (2021). Urban Mobility Innovation Index 2021. Available at htps://uitp.org/publicatons/urban-mobility-innovaton-index-2021

United Nations (2023). Explainer: How AI helps combat climate change. UN News. 3 November. Available at https://news.un.org/en/story/2023/11/1143187

United Nations Conference on Trade and Development (UNCTAD) (2023). UN Digital Government Awards celebrate excellence in online public services. 19 October. Available at https://unctad.org/news/un-digital-government-awards-celebrate-excellence-online-public-services

United Nations Environment Programme (UNEP (2021). New report reveals how infrastructure defines our climate. Press release. 12 October. Available at https://www.unep.org/news-and-stories/press-release/new-report-reveals-how-infrastructure-defines-our-climate#:~:text=The%20findings%20highlight%20that%20infrastructure,and%20the%20Sustainable%20Development%20Goals.

United Nations Environment Programme (UNEP) and Climate and Clean Air Coalition (2021). *Global Methane Assessment: Benefits and Costs of Mitigating Methane Emissions*. Nairobi. Available at https://www.unep.org/resources/report/global-methane-assessment-benefits-and-costs-mitigating-methane-emissions

United Nations Environment Programme (UNEP), and UN Climate Technology Centre and Network (CTCN) (2016). Strengthening Bangkok's Early Warning System to respond to climate induced flooding. 29 January. Available at https://www.ctc-n.org/technical-assistance/projects/strengthening-bangkok-s-early-warning-system-respond-climate-induced

__________ (2021). Climate risk assessment for subnational adaptation and establishment of a local climate information system for climate change adaptation (LISA) in Cambodia. 29 January. Available at https://www.ctc-n.org/technical-assistance/projects/climate-risk-assessment-subnational-adaptation-and-establishment

__________ (2022). Development of framework for real-time transport information systems for public transport i n Greater Dhaka. Available at https://www.ctc-n.org/technical-assistance/projects/development-framework-real-time-transport-information-systems-public

United Nations Economic and Social Commission for Asia and the Pacific (ESCAP) (2019). Asia-Pacific plan of action on space applications for sustainable development (2018–2030). Policy brief. 12 February. Available at https://www.unescap.org/resources/asia-pacific-plan-action-space-applications-sustainable-development-2018-2030

__________ (2020). New UN initiative to reduce plastic pollution from ASEAN cities. Press release, 5 May. Available at https://www.unescap.org/news/new-un-initiative-reduce-plastic-pollution-asean-cities

__________ (2021). *Review of Development in Transport in Asia and the Pacific: Towards Sustainable, Inclusive and Resilient Urban Passenger Transport in Asian Cities*. United Nations publications.

__________ (2022). Jakarta Ministerial Declaration on Space Applications for Sustainable Development in Asia and the Pacific. 26 October. ESCAP/MCSASD/2022/3/Add.1

__________ (2023a). *Asia-Pacific Disaster Report 2023: Seizing the Moment: Targeting Transformative Disaster Risk Resilience*. United Nations publication.

__________ (2023b). Regional Road Map to Support Regional Cooperation for the Wider Deployment of Sustainable Smart Transport Systems in Asia and the Pacific. Bangkok, Thailand.

__________ (2023c). *The Race to Net Zero: Accelerating Climate Action in Asia and the Pacific*. United Nations publication.

__________ (n.d.). Building the Pan Asia Partnership for Geospatial Air Pollution Information (PAPGAPI). Available at https://www.unescap.org/projects/papgapi;

United Nations University (2021). UNU-INWEH's World Flood Mapping Tool is one of 2021's "100 Greatest Innovations". Press release. 30 November. Available at https://unu.edu/press-release/unu-inwehs-world-flood-mapping-tool-one-2021s-100-greatest-innovations

__________ (n.d.). Introduction to Geospatial Data Analysis with ChatGPT and Google Earth Engine. Available at https://lc.unu.edu/courses/course-v1:UNU-INWEH+INWEH-20+2023_T4/about

Urban Redevelopment Authority (2024). Urban Transformations: Punggol Digital District. Available at https://www.ura.gov.sg/Corporate/Planning/Master-Plan/Master-Plan-2019/Urban-Transformations/Punggol-Digital-District

Waycott, Bonnie (2022). Can carbon mitigation strategies for aquafeeds help cut aquaculture's greenhouse gas emissions? Global Seafood Alliance, 12 December. Available at https://www.globalseafood.org/advocate/can-carbon-mitigation-strategies-for-aquafeeds-help-cut-aquacultures-greenhouse-gas-emissions/

World Steel Association (2024). Climate change and the production of iron and steel. Available at https://worldsteel.org/publications/policy-papers/climate-change-policy-paper/

World Bank (2024). Transport. Available at https://www.worldbank.org/en/topic/transport/overview#1

Yu, Ivy (2022). China tackles towering garbage heaps with artificial intelligence. *alizila News from Alibaba*, 8 April. Available at https://www.alizila.com/china-tackles-towering-garbage-heaps-with-artificial-intelligence/

Zhongwen, Huang (2021). AI in Urban Planning: 3 ways it will strengthen how we plan for the future. Urban Redevelopment Authority. 1 September. Available at https://www.ura.gov.sg/Corporate/Resources/Ideas-and-Trends/AI-in-Urban-Planning

Envisioning future scenarios

Asia-Pacific countries can use digital transformations to decouple economic growth from carbon emissions. Beyond a certain level of income, technological advances and productivity can reduce the levels of CO_2 production or at least slow the rate of emissions growth by applying a good package of policies. This chapter outlines three possible scenarios and the ways of steering transformations to address climate risks.

In the positive scenario, digital transformations reduce long-term carbon emissions by enhancing efficiency, innovation and connectivity. This will depend on key drivers that boost efficiency, enable substitution and leverage the combinatorial effect of emerging technologies. In the negative scenario, despite digital efficiency and innovations, total carbon emissions increase across the life cycle of digital devices and services, with the expansion of digital infrastructure, data centres and emerging technologies. The actual outcome and extent to which digital transformation contributes to climate action will depend on a country's technological advances and capacity, industrial structure and deliberate policy measures.

The interaction of digital transformation with climate change can result in multiple, complex outcomes (Figure 4-1). In broad terms, however, they can be encapsulated in three general future scenarios: positive, negative, or neutral. This chapter considers policy actions that avoid the negative outcomes and steer countries along more positive pathways.

FIGURE 4-1 The digital-growth-climate nexus can lead to one of three future scenarios

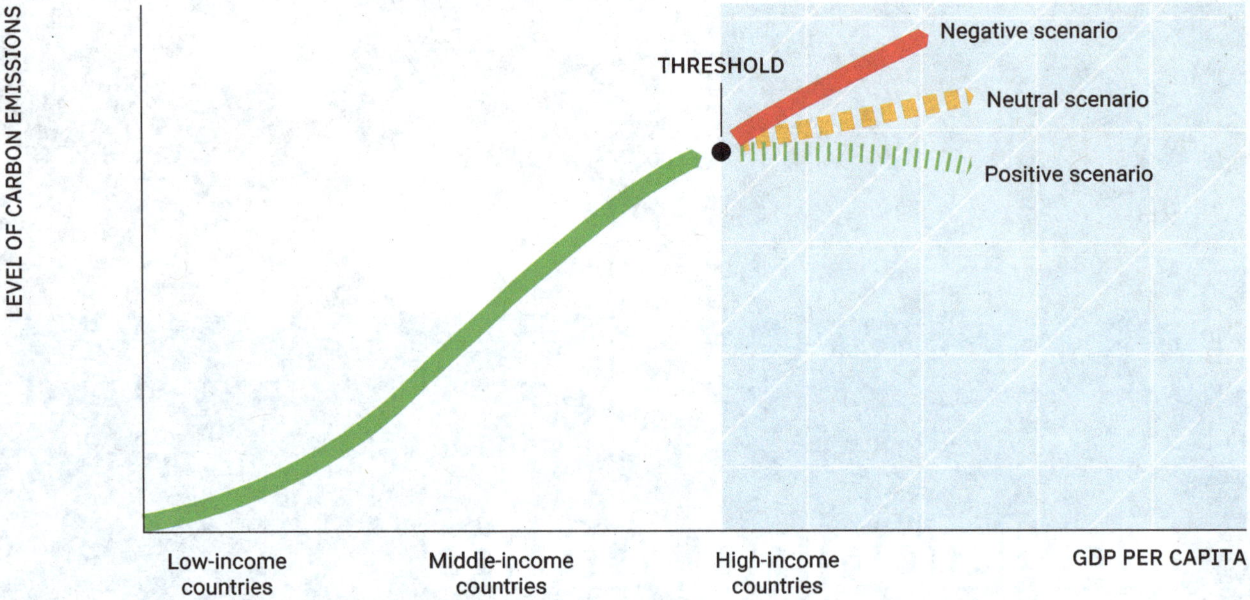

Source: ESCAP.

4.1 The positive scenario

Digital transformations reduce long-term carbon emissions by enhancing efficiency, finding solutions and promoting collaboration for climate mitigation and adaptation.

Digital transformations can mitigate GHG emissions, enhance adaptive capacity and boost resilience, particularly in the long run. Well-designed policies, regulatory frameworks and sustained investments in digital technologies, data and integrated digital platforms can support positive climate action and the implementation of SDG 13.

In 2020, energy industries were responsible for 34 per cent of emissions, raw materials industries accounted for 21 per cent and mobility industries for 19 per cent. According to Accenture and the World Economic Forum, widespread application of digital technology in these three sectors can enhance efficiency and foster low-carbon industrial ecosystems that could reduce their carbon emissions by up to 20 per cent, by 2050 (George, O'Regan, and Holst, 2022) (Figure 4-2).

FIGURE 4-2 **Benefits of digital solutions in high-emissions industries**

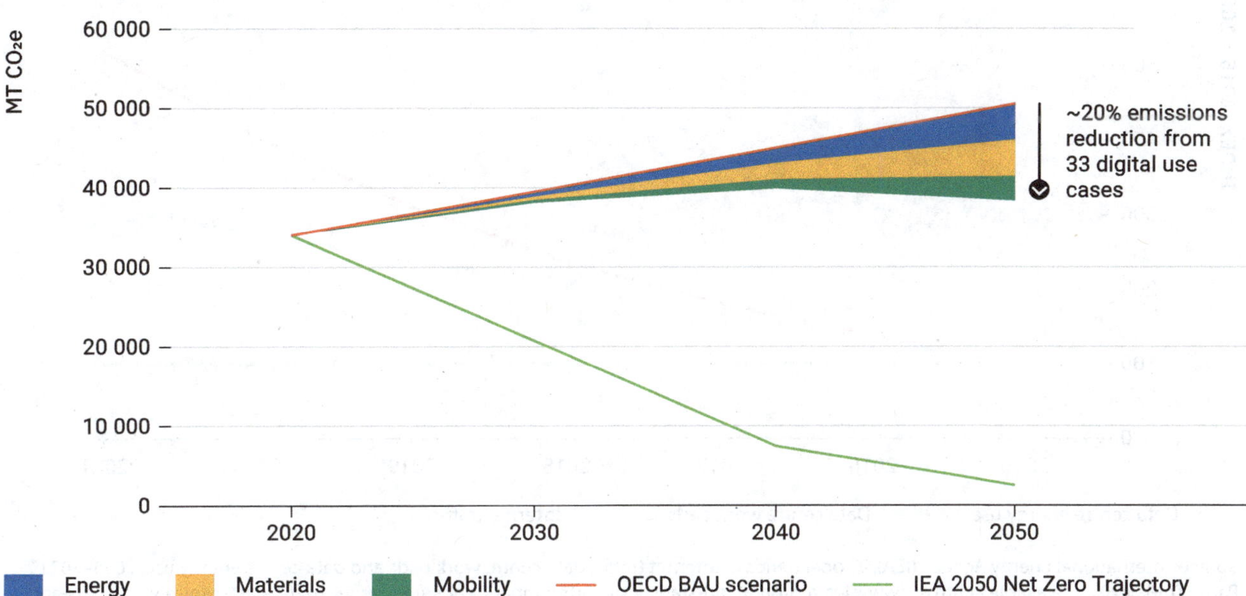

Source: Manju George, Karen O'Regan, and Alexander Holst, "Digital solutions can reduce global emissions by up to 20%. Here's how", World Economic Forum, 23 May 2022. Available at https://www.weforum.org/agenda/2022/05/how-digital-solutions-can-reduce-global-emissions/

The positive scenario will depend on key drivers that will boost efficiency, enable substitution and leverage the combinatorial effect of emerging technologies.

The efficiency effect: optimizing infrastructure and supply and demand

As demonstrated in Chapter 3, digital technologies can help improve efficiency and optimize existing infrastructure, as well as boost supply and demand across sectors. These include:

- *Smart grids:* Research in China has shown that applying smart grids in the manufacturing industry could reduce carbon emissions by over a quarter in optimal scenarios (Fu, Shi, and Zeng, 2021).
- *Digital twins:* These virtual models can be used to optimize infrastructure, particularly for energy. Research by EY shows that digital twins can help reduce the carbon footprint of an existing building by 50 per cent, including by measuring the optimized models on energy usage, reducing waste and improving indoor air quality within the building (Frearson, 2021).
- *Smart mobility:* Digital transformation in the mobility sector could decrease GHG emissions by 5 per cent by 2050 (George, O'Regan, and Holst, 2022).

Since 2010, despite the rapidly growing demand for digital products and services, carbon emissions have grown modestly. This is a consequence of improved energy efficiency, the integration of renewable energy and broader decarbonization of energy grids in every sector (IEA, n.d.b). According to the IEA, the deployment of digital technologies and big data could save $80 billion per year, or around 5 per cent of total world annual power generation costs (IEA, 2017).

Data centres use vast amounts of energy and global Internet traffic has tripled since 2015, yet data-centre energy use remains fairly flat. This reflects a shift to hyperscale data centres and the use of digital technologies that have contributed to greater energy efficiency.

FIGURE 4-3 **Global trends in Internet traffic, data centre workloads and data centre energy use**

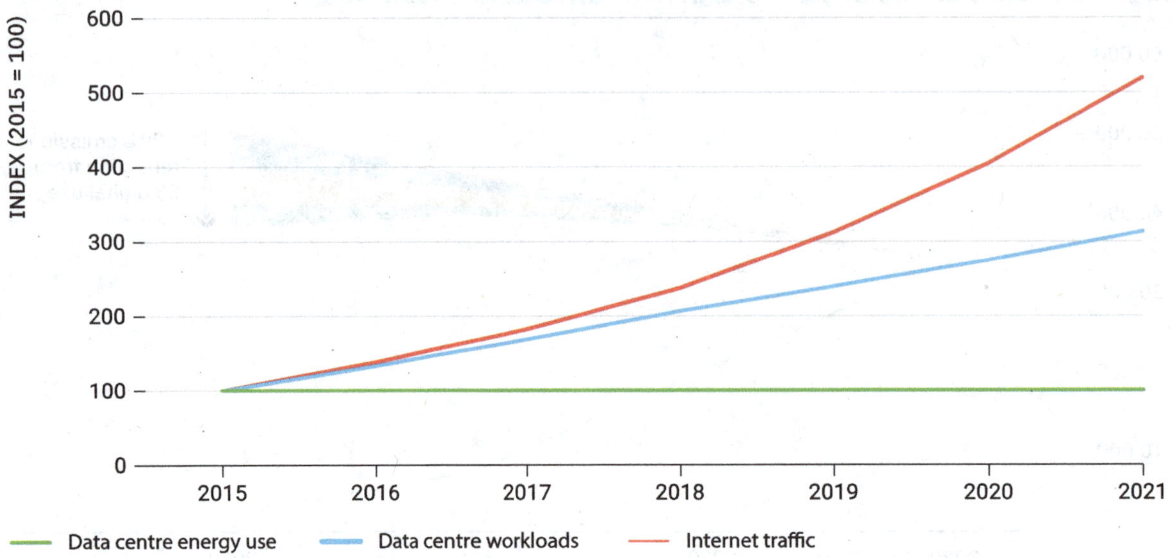

Source: International Energy Agency (IEA), "Global trends in internet traffic, data centre workloads and data centre energy use, 2015–2021", Paris, 27 May 2019. Available at https://www.iea.org/data-and-statistics/charts/global-trends-in-internet-traffic-data-centre-workloads-and-data-centre-energy-use-2015-2021

The substitution effect: reducing physical needs and processes

Digital technologies enable physical needs and processes to be substituted with digital and virtual alternatives, contributing to both dematerialization and decarbonization that help shrink carbon footprints.

The COVID-19 pandemic triggered, or at least sped up, the virtualization of business processes and move to remote working, thereby fundamentally changing the ways in which individuals, companies and governments operate and communicate with each other. At the same time, the pandemic temporarily cut overall production and consumption. As a result, in April 2020, compared to peak 2019 levels, during the COVID-19 lockdowns, dramatic changes in mobility, production and consumption patterns temporarily reduced global carbon emissions by 17 per cent (Le Quéré, and others, 2020).

Meanwhile, by making more processes digital and using electronic documentation cut the demand for physical documents and paper. This is encouraging news for the climate; a reduction in the demand for wood and the resulting slowing deforestation, while avoiding huge quantities of unrecycled paper from going to landfills. In addition, digital service platforms save costs and boost efficiency through enabling greater connectivity.

The combinatorial effect: the rise of AI and greater connectivity

Ever-changing interactions and synergies between foundational and emerging technologies, particularly the rise of AI, are accelerating the advance of energy-saving and emissions-reduction technologies. These present tremendous opportunities to accelerate the transition towards low-carbon infrastructure and renewable energy sources, and tread on the path toward efficient, interconnected energy systems and net-zero carbon emissions.

Transformational technologies are also altering human and societal behaviours and interactions, including organizational and work processes, household consumption patterns and business models (Teufel, and Sprus, 2020).

Empirical observation: Digital-climate-growth nexus of ASEAN countries, Nordic countries and G7 members

Based on the digital-growth-climate nexus, discussed in Chapter 2, the relationships between digital transformation (individual Internet usage), income (GDP per capita) and carbon emissions (GHG per capita) were analysed for ASEAN countries, Nordic countries and G7 members.

Figure 4-4 observes that for ASEAN countries, generally the higher the per capita GDP, the higher the per capita GHG emissions. The exception is Singapore, a promising example which indicates that beyond a certain threshold of GDP per capita, GHG emissions per capita may decline. This is supported by other research which shows that in the long run digitalization can help decarbonization (Barrutiabengoa, and others, 2022).

FIGURE 4-4 GHG emissions and GDP with average Internet usage in ASEAN countries, 2011–2022

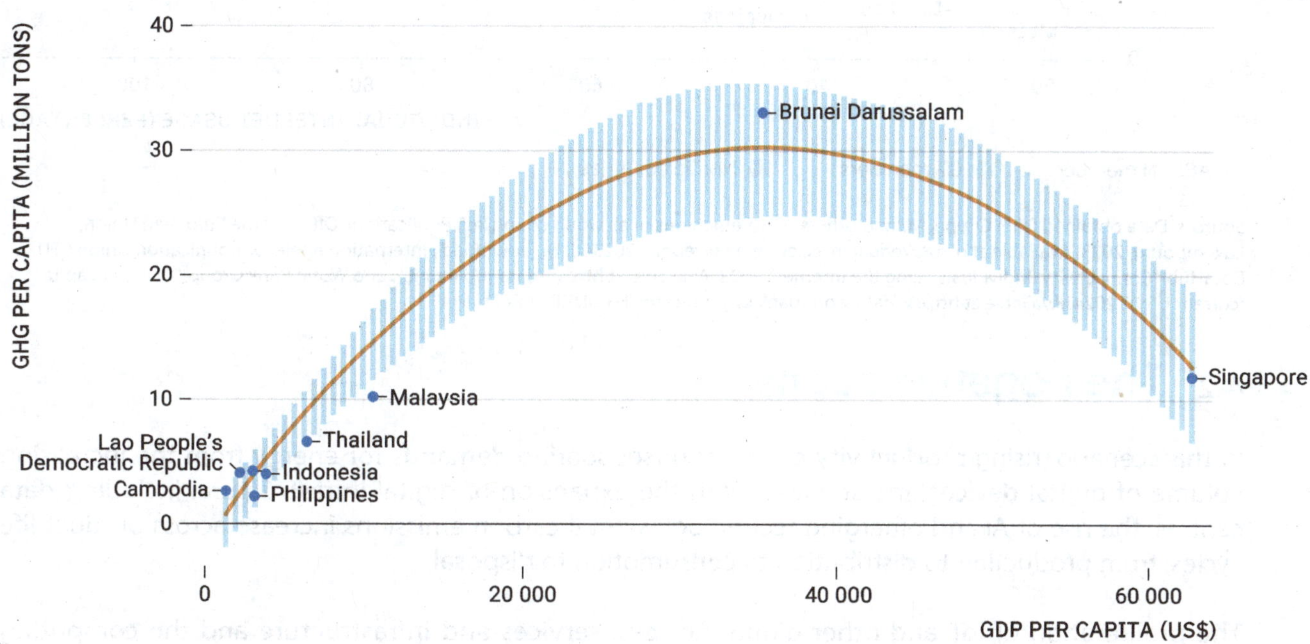

Source: Created by ESCAP, on STATA using data obtained from Crippa, M., and others, "GHG emissions of all world countries", Publications Office of the European Union, Luxembourg, 2023. Available at https://edgar.jrc.ec.europa.eu/report_2023#data_download ; International Telecommunication Union (ITU) DataHub, "Connectivity: Individuals using the Internet", 2023. Available at https://datahub.itu.int/ ; and World Bank Group, "GDP per capita (current US$)", 2024. Available at https://data.worldbank.org/indicator/NY.GDP.PCAP.CD

Note: Values fitted at 95 per cent Confidence Interval (CI): These are the range of values that we expect our estimate to fall between 95 per cent of the time if we run our tests again or re-sample the population in the same way.

This observation is reinforced when the analysis is extended to the Nordic and G7 economies. Nordic countries have higher average incomes than ASEAN countries, as well as greater average Internet connectivity, yet they have lower per capita GHG emissions. G7 countries, which have high Internet use, also generally have lower per capita carbon emissions (Figure 4-5).

However, there are outliers, notably Brunei Darussalam, Canada and the United States of America which have higher per capita carbon emissions than other countries at similar income levels. This highlights the importance of resolute national policies, regulatory frameworks, industry structures and sociocultural behaviours that can steer the climate change trajectory in a positive direction.

FIGURE 4-5   GHG emissions per capita and individual Internet usage across ASEAN countries, Nordic countries and G7 members

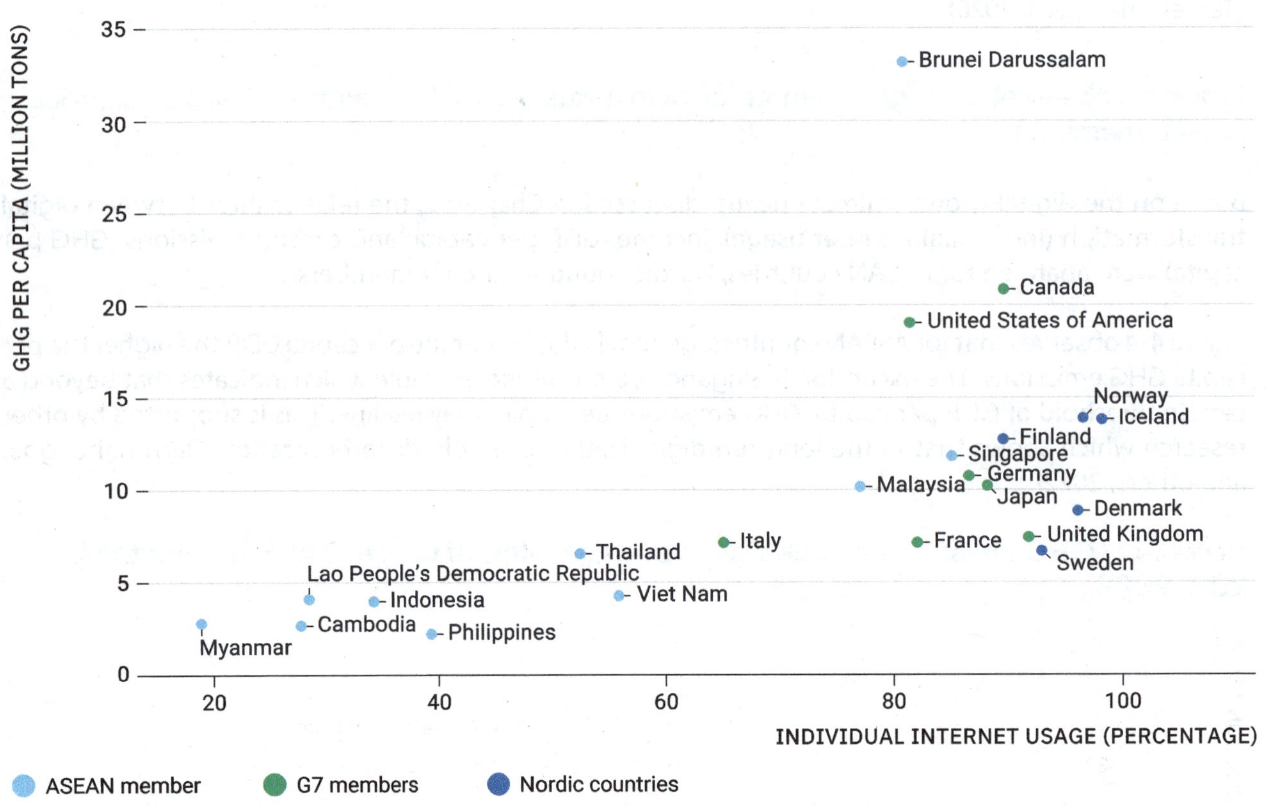

Sources: Data obtained from Crippa, M., and others, "GHG emissions of all world countries", Publications Office of the European Union, Luxembourg, 2023. Available at https://edgar.jrc.ec.europa.eu/report_2023#data_download ; International Telecommunication Union (ITU) DataHub, "Connectivity: Individuals using the Internet", 2023. Available at https://datahub.itu.int/ ; and World Bank Group, "GDP per capita (current US$)", 2024. Available at https://data.worldbank.org/indicator/NY.GDP.PCAP.CD

4.2   The negative scenario

In this scenario, rising productivity does not offset soaring demands for energy from the increasing volume of digital devices and services. With the expansion of digital infrastructure, including data centres, the rise of AI and emerging technologies, total carbon emissions increase across product life cycles; from production to distribution to consumption to disposal.

The proliferation of IoT and other digital devices, services and infrastructure and the computing demands of AI add to the load of data centres, in particular old and low-efficiency data centres, with corresponding surges in demand for electricity and rising carbon emissions. The carbon footprint of individual devices or services may be shrinking, but the huge number of digital devices adds to the overall carbon footprint of rapidly advancing digital societies, while increasing the challenges to sustainability and the circular economy.

Proliferation of digital devices and data centres with the demands of AI

Between 2023 and 2026, energy demands of the AI industry are expected to increase at least ten-fold. Between 2022 and 2026, total electricity consumption by data centres could increase from 460 TWh to more than 1,000 TWh. By 2030, data centres could require 30 gigawatts of additional capacity.

Data centre electricity use in Ireland, for example, has more than tripled since 2015, while in Denmark, it is projected to rise six times by 2030, by which time it will account for almost 15 per cent of the country's electricity use (IEA, n.d.a.).

Even in this scenario, the generation of energy from renewables is set to expand (Figure 4-6), and renewables and other low-emission sources could meet the world's growth in energy demand by 2026. Nevertheless, the overall energy consumption of data centres is likely to continue growing, primarily from non-renewable resources (Statista, n.d.a).

FIGURE 4-6   Projected changes in global electricity generation, 2022–2030

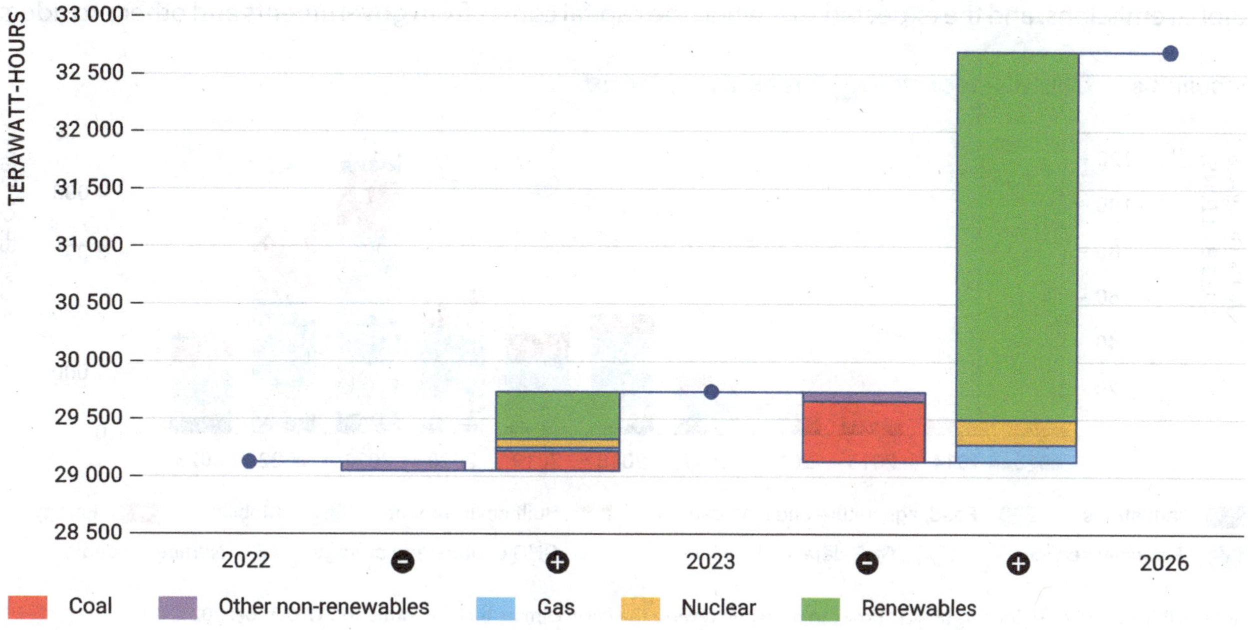

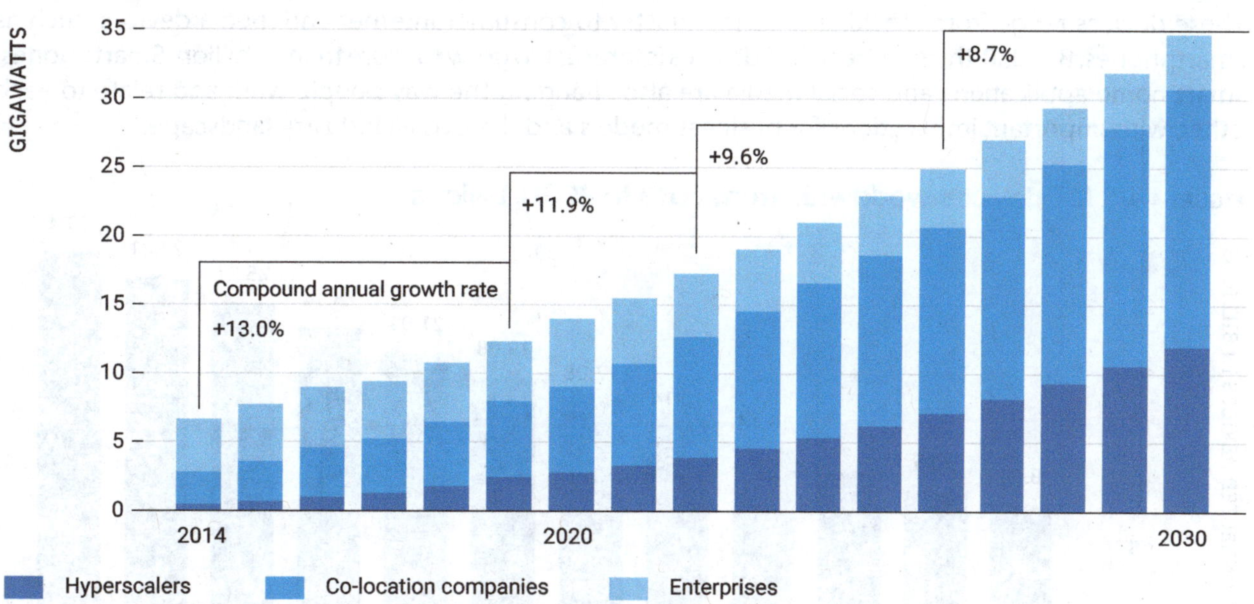

Source: International Energy Agency, "Electricity 2024" (Paris, 2024). Available at https://www.iea.org/reports/electricity-2024

The digital economy thus confronts the dual challenge of meeting the increasing energy demands of inclusive digital societies and addressing mounting climate concerns.

FIGURE 4-7   Data-centre power consumption in the United States of America, by providers and enterprises, 2014–2030, gigawatts

Source: Srini Bangalore and others, "Investing in the rising data center economy", McKinsey & Company, McKinsey's Technology, Media & Telecommunications Practice, 17 January 2023. Available at https://www.mckinsey.com/industries/technology-media-and-telecommunications/our-insights/investing-in-the-rising-data-center-economy

Uneven investment in climate technologies

According to PricewaterhouseCoopers' (PwC) analysis, between 2021 and 2023, due to market conditions, investments in climate technology have fallen (Plasschaert, and Barabas, 2023) (Figure 4-8). On the other hand, S&P Global Commodity Insights forecasts that between 2023 and 2024 clean energy technology investments will increase by 10 to 20 per cent to nearly $800 billion. Generally, investment is uneven; little private capital investment goes into those sectors that generate the biggest shares of global emissions, and the expectation is when the capital comes from governments and other providers.

FIGURE 4-8   **Climate technology investment trend**

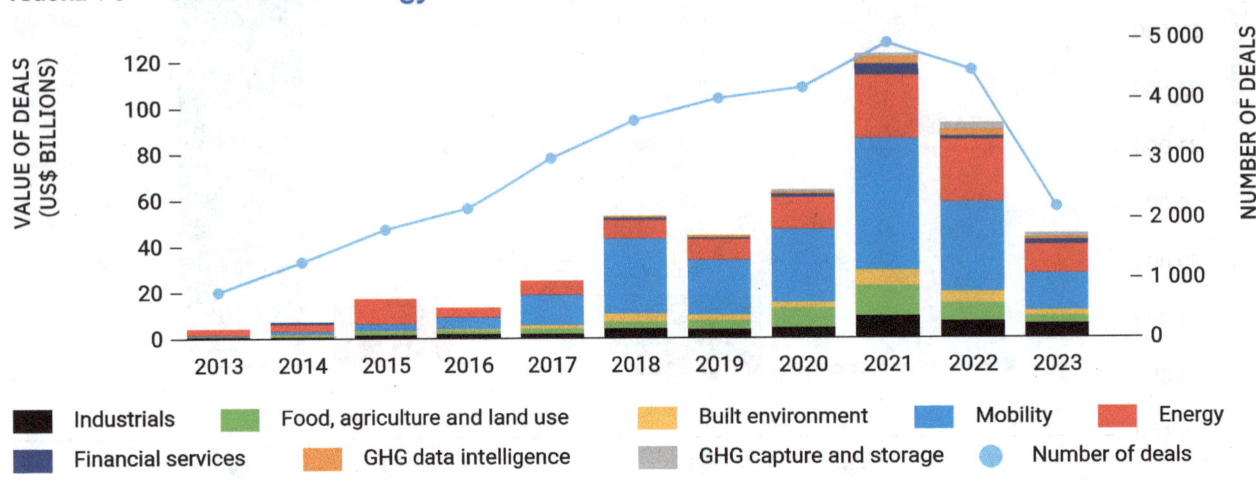

Source: PricewaterhouseCoopers (PwC), "How can the world reverse the fall in climate tech investment?", 17 October 2023. Available at https://www.pwc.com/gx/en/issues/esg/state-of-climate-tech-2023-investment.html

End-user demand increases carbon footprints

Consumer preferences, choices and behaviours are being reshaped by digital connectivity and the IoT. As indicated in Figure 4-9, the number of IoT-connected devices worldwide has steadily increased and forecasts show a continued upward trend, projected to be 29 billion by 2030.

These devices range from machine tools in industry to consumer Internet and media devices, such as smartphones. By 2030, the number of IoT devices is forecast to grow to more than 17 billion. Smartphones, smart home applications and social media are also changing the way people work and relate to each other, with important implications for business models and the overall industry landscape.

FIGURE 4-9   **IoT devices worldwide from 2019 to 2030, billions**

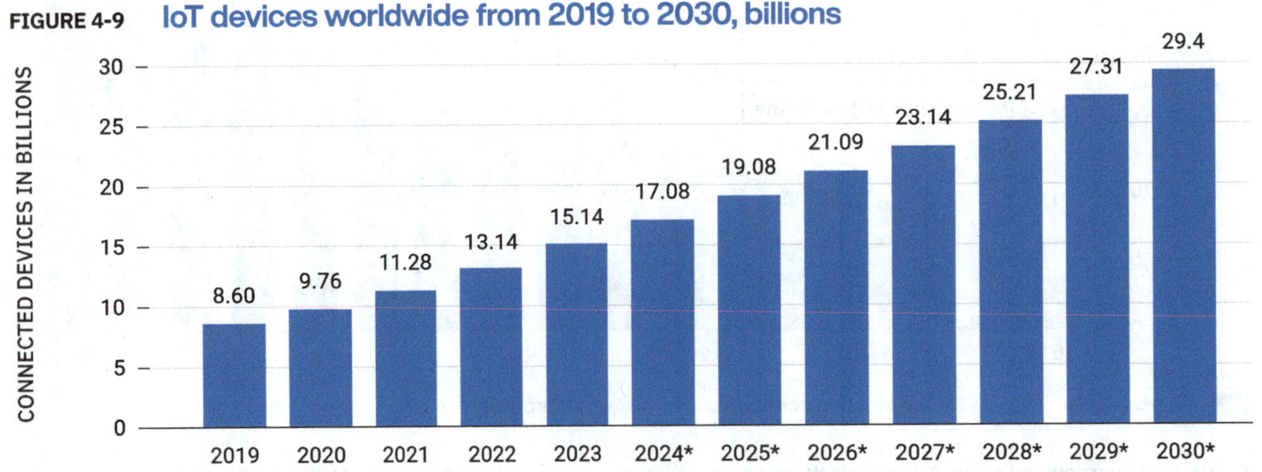

Source: Statista, "Number of Internet of Things (IoT) connections worldwide from 2022 to 2023, with forecasts from 2024–2033 (in billions), n.d. Available at https://www.statista.com/statistics/1183457/iot-connected-devices-worldwide

Note: * data are projections.

In 2015, connected household appliances consumed 360 TWh, accounting for 13 per cent of total household electricity consumption. By 2040, this proportion could increase to 50 per cent as smart home applications and technology reshape living spaces, offering greater convenience and more integrated and efficient home ecosystems (Figure 4-10).

FIGURE 4-10 **Electricity consumption of household appliances and other small-plug loads**

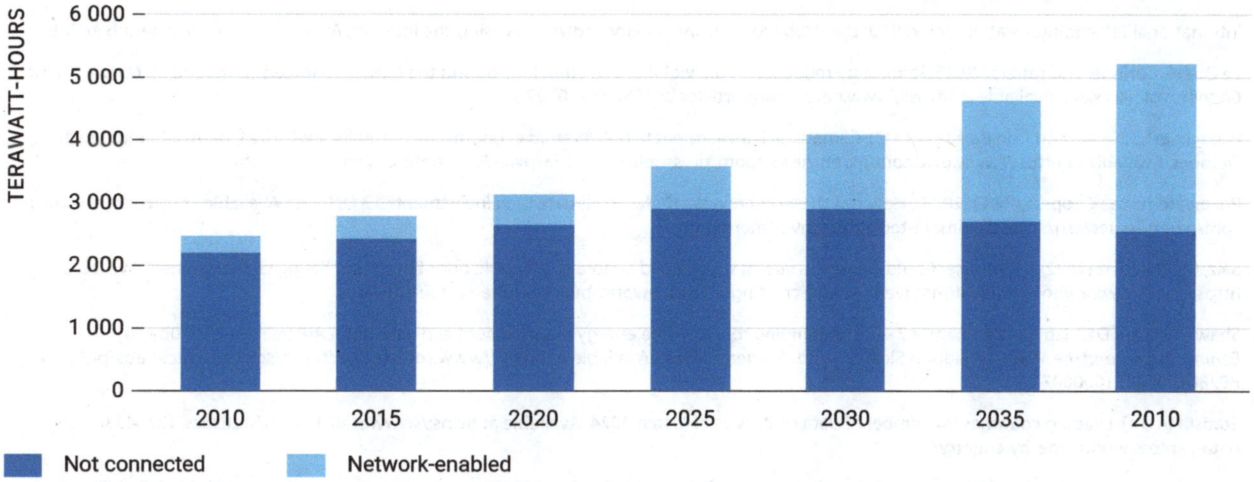

Source: Damian Shaw-Williams, "Chapter 7 -The expanding role of home energy management ecosystem: An Australian case study", In *Behind and Beyond the Meter*, Fereidoon Sioshansi, ed. (Academic Press, 2020). Available at https://www.sciencedirect.com/science/article/abs/pii/B9780128199510000074

4.3 The neutral scenario

In this case, the net impact of digital transformation on climate change is neither positive nor negative. Despite the positive contribution of digital technologies to climate action, the increasing energy use and resulting carbon emissions from the digital economy offset the benefits of digital transformation for climate action. With various factors cancelling each other out, the result is broadly neutral.

Whether digital transformations help or hinder climate action has been a subject of debate within the scientific community. But it is clear that the extent to which digital transformation contributes to climate action will depend on a country's technological advances and capacity, industrial structure and deliberate policy measures. Some of the measures that countries can adopt are summarized in the next chapter.

Chapter 4 References

Bangalore, Srini, and others (2023). Investing in the rising data center economy. McKinsey & Company,McKinsey's Technology, Media & Telecommunications Practice. 17 January. Available at https://www.mckinsey.com/industries/technology-media-and-telecommunications/our-insights/investing-in-the-rising-data-center-economy

Barrutiabengoa, Joxe Mari, and others (2022). How do digitalization and decarbonization efforts interact? BBVA Research. 26 May. Available at https://www.bbvaresearch.com/wp-content/uploads/2022/05/How-do-digitalization-and-decarbonization-efforts-interact_2T22.pdf

Crippa, M., and others (2023). GHG emissions of all world countries. Publications Office of the European Union, Luxembourg. Available at https://edgar.jrc.ec.europa.eu/report_2023#data_download

Frearson, Amy (2021). Digital twins are "big driver" towards net-zero cities say experts. Dezeen. 7 September. Available at https://www.dezeen.com/2021/09/07/digital-twins-climate-change-net-zero-cities/

Fu, H., Y. Shi, and Y. Zeng (2021). Estimating Smart Grid's Carbon Emission Reduction Potential in China's Manufacturing Industry Based on Decomposition Analysis. *Frontiers in Energy Research*, vol. 9 (June). Available at https://doi.org/10.3389/fenrg.2021.681244

George, Manju, Karen O'Regan, and Alexander Holst (2022). Digital solutions can reduce global emissions by up to 20%. Here's how. World Economic Forum. 23 May. Available at https://www.weforum.org/agenda/2022/05/how-digital-solutions-can-reduce-global-emissions/

International Energy Agency (IEA) (2017). *Digitalisation and Energy*. Paris. Available at https://www.iea.org/reports/digitalisation-and-energy

__________ (2019) Global trends in internet traffic, data centre workloads and data centre energy use, 2015–2021. Paris. 27 May. Available at https://www.iea.org/data-and-statistics/charts/global-trends-in-internet-traffic-data-centre-workloads-and-data-centre-energy-use-2015-2021

__________ (2024). *Electricity 2024*. Paris. Available at https://www.iea.org/reports/electricity-2024

__________ (n.d.a.). Data Centres and Data Transmission Networks. Available at https://www.iea.org/energy-system/buildings/data-centres-and-data-transmission-networks

__________ (n.d.b.). Digitalisation. Available at https://www.iea.org/energy-system/decarbonisation-enablers/digitalisation

International Telecommunication Union (ITU) DataHub (2023). Connectivity: Individuals using the Internet. Available at https://datahub.itu.int/

Le Quéré, Corinne, and others (2020). Temporary reduction in daily global CO_2 emissions during the COVID-19 forced confinement. *Nature Climate Change*, vol. 10 (May). Available at https://www.nature.com/articles/s41558-020-0797-x

Plasschaert, Andrea, and Dan Barabas (2023). Climate tech investment falls 40% amid economic uncertainity: PwC 2023 State of Climate Tech. 17 October. Available at https://www.pwc.com/gx/en/news-room/press-releases/2023/pwc-2023-state-of-climate-tech.html

Pricewaterhouse Coopers (PwC) (2023). How can the world reverse thefall in climate tech investment? 17 October. Available at https://www.pwc.com/gx/en/issues/esg/state-of-climate-tech-2023-investment.html

Sáiz, Beatriz Sanz (2022). Metaverse: Could creating a virtual world build a more sustainable one? Ernest and Young Global Limited. Available at https://www.ey.com/en_gl/digital/metaverse-could-creating-a-virtual-world-build-a-more-sustainable-one

Shaw-Williams, Damian (2020). Chapter 7 – The expanding role of home energy management ecosystem: An Australian case study. In *Behind and Beyond the Meter*, Fereidoon Sioshansi, ed. Academic Press. Available at https://www.sciencedirect.com/science/article/abs/pii/B9780128199510000074

Statista (n.d.a). Leading countries by number of data centers as of March 2024. Available at https://www.statista.com/statistics/1228433/data-centers-worldwide-by-country/

__________ (n.d.b). Number of Internet of Things (IoT) connections worldwide from 2022 to 2023, with forecasts from 2024–2033 (in billions). Available at https://www.statista.com/statistics/1183457/iot-connected-devices-worldwide

Teufel, Benjamin, and Carment Sprus (2020). How digitalization acts as a driver of decarbonization. Ernest and Young Global Limited. Available at https://www.ey.com/en_ch/decarbonization/how-digitization-acts-as-a-driver-of-decarbonization

World Bank Group (2024). GDP per capita (current US$). Available at https://data.worldbank.org/indicator/NY.GDP.PCAP.CD

Digital destinations: key findings and policy recommendations

Digital technologies have brought multiple economic and social benefits, yet their implications for climate change are not immediately obvious or too specifically considered depending on various factors. This *Report* has tried to draw attention to the need to redress the balance and trigger the digital-growth-climate nexus.

Under these circumstances, although societies and economies are being reshaped by digital transformations and climate change, digital technologies can be strong allies of climate action, alter the climate change trajectory and help decouple economic growth from carbon emissions. Building on ESCAP's Digital Transformation Framework, this chapter proposes recommendations for its five pillars: infrastructure and network; government; business; people; and ecosystems.

5.1 Key findings

1 · **Digital transformations and climate change are reshaping societies and economies.**

Digital transformation goes beyond digitization or digitalization; it is a paradigm shift that profoundly impacts all sectors and reweaves the whole fabric of society. While climate change remains the defining challenge of our time, its trajectory can be redirected by digital transformations that offer dramatic productivity gains, economies of scale, cost savings and innovative solutions for climate mitigation and adaptation.

2 **Digital technologies are strong allies of climate action.**

Digital innovations, big data and AI-driven analytics are increasingly deepening our understanding of the causes and patterns of climate change. Innovative solutions are emerging through technological developments, including AI, blockchain, IoT, geospatial technologies and cloud data architectures. They can be used to optimize existing infrastructure, systems and production, while reshaping consumption patterns. Digital solutions can also offer breakthroughs across infrastructure, government, mobility, industry and trade. In addition, they can benefit agriculture and biodiversity ecosystems and build adaptive capacity in reducing disaster risks.

3 **Economic growth, driven by digital transformation, can alter the climate change trajectory and thereby provide practical policies and strategies.**

Adding a climate change dimension to ESCAP's Digital Transformation Index Framework helps to zero in on the digital-growth-climate nexus. This demonstrates that in the early stages of development carbon emissions tend to rise, but as technology advances, beyond a certain level of income, the level of carbon emissions generally begins to decline, as does the rate of emissions growth. Moreover, the higher the level of technological progress, the higher can be the rate of decline, thereby offering a pathway to sustainable economic growth while addressing climate change (Figure 5-1).

4 **Economic growth can be decoupled from carbon emissions in digitally advanced, high-income countries.**

Singapore, the Republic of Korea and the Nordic countries are among the most digitally advanced countries in ESCAP's Digital Transformation Index. They have been able to grow their economies while reducing carbon emissions per capita and strengthening adaptive capacity. Since 2000, globally, as GDPs have risen there has been a notable reduction in GHG emissions per capita, suggesting that technological development can be leveraged to decouple economic growth and climate change. Developing countries, are at earlier stages: while undergoing digital transformations they still often have high energy intensities, due to rapid industrialization and urbanization, and the need to build extensive infrastructure.

5   Future scenarios, positive or negative, will depend on an interplay of factors.

The extent to which digital transformation contributes to climate action will depend on the interplay between a country's technological capacity and progress, its industrial structure and the deliberate policy measures it takes to harness the benefits of digital transformation for climate mitigation and adaptation. As indicated in Figure 5-2, even if technological advances lead to a reduction in carbon emissions, the rate of decline will be different depending on the country's technological level, its regulatory policies, industrial structure and sociocultural context.

FIGURE 5-1   The digital-growth-climate nexus

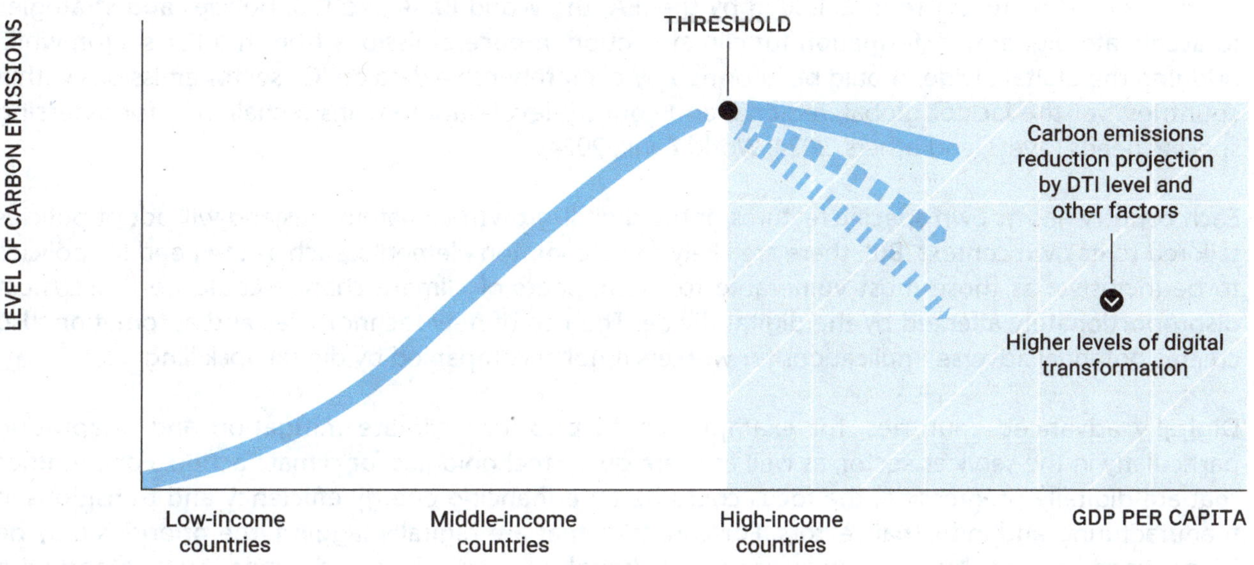

Source: ESCAP.

FIGURE 5-2   Three scenarios of the digital-growth-climate nexus

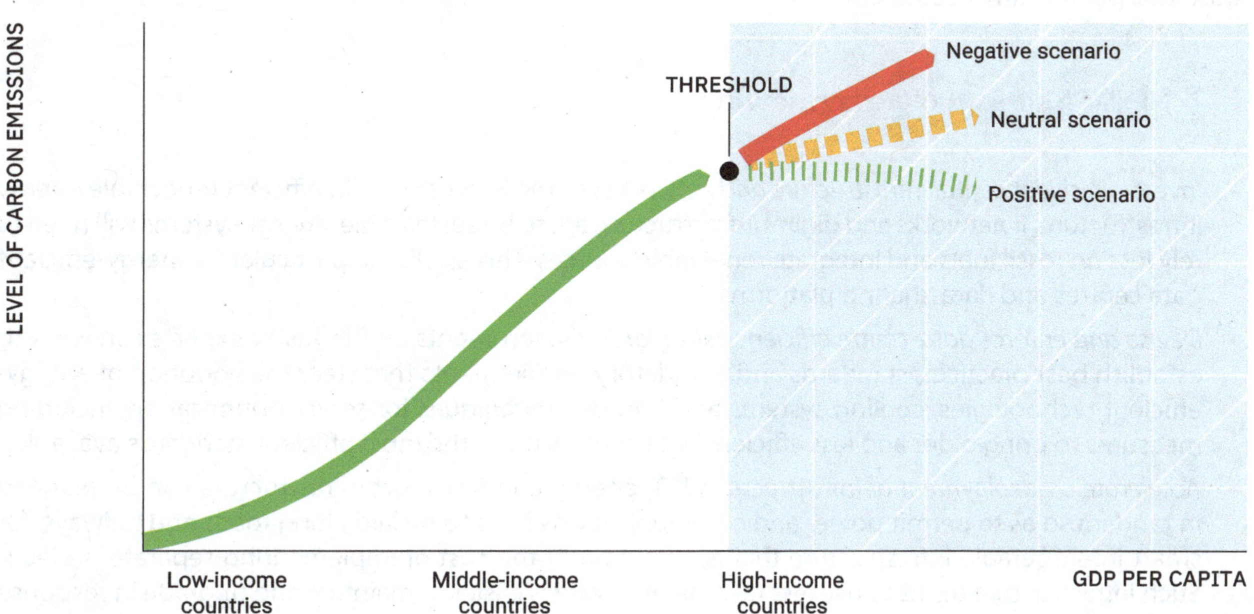

Source: ESCAP.

5.2 Recommendations

Across Asia and the Pacific, countries differ widely in their levels of technological capacity, regulatory policies, industry structures, existing infrastructure, and their digital culture and behaviour patterns. The region faces several barriers to the adoption of digital solutions, including the lack of adequate digital infrastructure, particularly in rural and remote areas, the gender digital divide in the use of Internet and mobile devices, disparities in digital and technological skills across demographics, as well as the costs and challenges of accessing sophisticated technologies between digitally advanced and developing countries.

As highlighted by recent reports issued by the IEA, the World Bank and ITU, policies and strategies to accelerate digital transformation for climate action, reduce emissions from the ICT sector, while bridging the digital divide, should be informed by comprehensive data on ICT sector emissions within countries, yet the lack of global, regional and country-level data remains a challenge for assessing specific needs (Ayers, and others, 2024; World Bank, 2024).

Each country has its own specific features of the digital-growth-climate nexus and will adopt policies tailored to its own context. But, there are likely to be common elements, such as the need for policies to be inclusive, as those most vulnerable to the impacts of climate change could be those most disproportionately affected by the digital divide. The rise of new technologies and automation also creates potential adverse implications for workers if not accompanied by digital upskilling.

Digitally advanced countries, for example, could prioritize climate mitigation and adaptation particularly in the services sector, as well as share green technologies for climate action. For countries that are digitally progressing, the focus could be on enhancing energy efficiency and transitions in manufacturing and industrial sectors. For countries that are digitally lagging, the priorities may be innovations in agriculture and investments in digital infrastructures and connectivity, along with measures for bridging digital divides. Building on ESCAP's Digital Transformation Framework, the following recommendations are proposed for its five pillars: infrastructure and network; government; business; people; and ecosystem.

 **Pillar 1: Infrastructure and network**

- *Invest in resilient digital infrastructure and network systems,* in particular, in efficient renewable energy infrastructure. If networks and digital infrastructure are to be sustainable, energy systems will need to rely less on fossil fuels and integrate renewable sources. This applies in particular to energy-efficient data centres and data-sharing platforms.
- *Devise and enforce data-centre efficiency standards.* Governments and industry experts can work to establish best practices, standards and mandatory requirements that steer the adoption of energy-efficient technologies, cooling systems and improve techniques for server optimization, including measures to bring older and less efficient data centres up to the most efficient standards available.
- *Accelerate co-deployment of infrastructure.* ICT, energy and transport infrastructure can be planned in tandem so as to permit power and communications lines to be laid along roads and railways, for smart interoperable infrastructure that is a fraction of the cost of implementing separate projects. Such infrastructure tends to use less raw material, and is easier to maintain and upgrade in response to environmental demands and technological advances.
- *Promote open-source applications, and share design, code and software* to foster innovation and technology transfer.
- *Ensure that infrastructure deployed is modular and interoperable* as doing so will allow for easier upgrading in response to environmental demands and technological advancements. Such flexibility also enhances resilience and reduces material used, thereby promoting sustainable and cost-effective digital development.

 Pillar 2: Government

- *Integrate and coordinate digital, climate and economic plans, strategies and processes.* Given the digital-growth-climate nexus, coordinating relevant ministries and national policy and strategic planning processes can harmonize digital transformations and encourage economic growth and climate action across all sectors. In the process, policymakers across all domains learn, apply lessons and deepen their understanding of how digital transformations affect climate change. This can include tools to assess the impacts of digital transformations on indicators and targets of SDG 13.

- *Invest in research and development.* Increase investment in green digital hardware and software to find new ways to improve energy efficiency, in particular, including the shared development, production and use of AI for climate action and disaster risk reduction.

- *Keep software and data in the public domain.* Open-source software is an important form of public goods. Governments can also ensure open access to government data to encourage collecting, sharing and managing high-quality good data related to mitigation and adaptation, including easy access to national and global research and academic databases by solving IP issues and providing access means.

- *Governments are encouraged to address Internet coverage gaps for digital solutions to reach vulnerable communities* by strengthening regulatory frameworks together with policy measures, such as investment-friendly spectrum policies, tax incentives and universal service funds, and incentivize mobile network operators to invest in connectivity infrastructures.

- *Strengthen the strategic foresight and capacity of government officials.* Current and future generations of policymakers will need the skills to design new plans, projects and programmes that harness the benefits of emerging technologies by learning good practices and lessons learned of digitally advanced countries.

- *Integrate digital governance principles and safeguards in digital solutions for climate action*, including ensuring ethical use of digital data, building trust in the use of digital applications to address climate change and mitigate risks associated with the use of digital technologies.

 Pillar 3: Business

- *Boost investments in low-carbon markets, green and climate technologies and renewable energy infrastructures by filling the gap between short-term investment and long-term return.* To produce profitable products and services, the business sector should be able to rely on strong regulatory frameworks with built-in flexibilities to accommodate rapid technological changes, supported by incentivizing policies. They can target emerging technologies, such as generative AI, advanced robotics and carbon capture technologies.

- *Enhance business sustainability by adopting lower carbon production and consumption processes* and leverage digital technologies to optimize efficiency. Such actions should go in line with promoting sustainability across business strategies and actions, including integrating environmental, social and governance metrics, to help reduce adverse environmental and social impacts. It is critical to build a system that gives prospective national or international investors the confidence that they can achieve both a stable return and increase their social contribution toward carbon reduction.

 Pillar 4: People

- *Raise public awareness and encourage behavioural change.* Greater awareness of the environmental issues related to the use of digital devices and applications can encourage more sustainable digital practices. This includes powering down digital devices when not in use and recycling e-waste. Consumers can also delete unwanted data in cloud space so as to reduce energy consumption.

- *Build lifelong digital skills.* Much of the world's activity is becoming 'digital by default'. If societies are to be fully empowered to engage in a digital future, the all of society should be able to rely on lifelong educational programmes. Governments and business can also invest in digital skills for youth, regularly retrain and upskill workers to enhance their employability, encourage digital entrepreneurship, and ensure that digital skills empower ageing populations to meaningfully engage in the digital world.

 **Pillar 5: Ecosystem**

- *Build enabling environments for public-private partnerships.* Governments and businesses can collaborate on investments in climate technologies, for both short-term returns and shareholder value, as well as long-term societal benefits and environmental sustainability. This may include subsidies, tax cuts and long-term, low-interest loans to promote investments in low-carbon and resilient technologies and devices.
- *Strengthen regulatory frameworks and standards.* Regulations can guide investment in green digital infrastructure and clean grid infrastructure and require data centres to use more renewable energy. Frameworks should also require more open public access and data-sharing.
- *Strengthen financing systems.* Global and regional financing systems can support the transition from carbon-intensive to carbon-reduction manufacturing structures.
- *Strengthen regional platforms and initiatives.* The Asia-Pacific Information Superhighway Initiative (APIS) is enabling governments to share their visions, technology and good practices and build partnerships for digital and climate actions.
- *Develop a repository of best practices.* The more digitally advanced countries can offer case studies for the digital-growth-climate nexus to share good practices and promote South-South and Triangular cooperation.
- *Leverage existing cooperation networks.* The Asia-Pacific Information Superhighway platform, for example, allows researchers, policymakers and businesses to build networks to share the latest research and ensure that this informs policy decisions and business practices, leading to more coordinated digital actions against climate change.
- *Strengthen the data ecosystem for informed policy decisions and monitoring.* In this regard, strengthened availability of open-access data as well as data interoperability are essential in facilitating the use of data, while the development of tools to measure the impacts of digital transformation actions on SDG 13, at the target and indicator levels, remains important.

5.3 Regional cooperation for digital innovation

Countries in Asia and the Pacific have an unparalleled opportunity to use digital transformations to pursue sustainable and inclusive economic growth and mitigate climate risks in a zero-sum game. With the transboundary nature of economic, social and environmental challenges beyond the ability of any single country to address, regional cooperation is imperative for governments across the region to build an inclusive digital future, extend connectivity to all and harness new technologies to confront the challenges of climate change and environmental degradation.

In May 2023, the 79th session of the Economic and Social Commission for Asia and the Pacific, through Resolution 79/10, committed to strengthening digital cooperation and inclusion through the Action Plan for implementing the Asia-Pacific Information Superhighway (APIS) Initiative 2022–2026. The APIS initiative aims to foster digital connectivity and applications and serve as a platform for digital cooperation, dialogue and partnerships between governments, businesses and other stakeholders.

In addition, at the 80th session of the Commission, through resolution 80/1, ESCAP members and associate members welcomed the convening of the Asia-Pacific Ministerial Conference on Digital Inclusion and Transformation, organized by ESCAP and hosted by the Government of Kazakhstan on 3–5 September 2024, in Astana. The ministerial conference is expected to embark on a visionary and ambitious blueprint for regional digital cooperation, to accelerate the implementation of the Sustainable Development Goals and regional technology initiatives.

Only in a spirit of collaboration can countries within Asia and the Pacific leverage the opportunities presented by digital innovations to bring about transformative, positive change that will support national and regional efforts to avert a climate catastrophe.

Chapter 5 References

Ayers, Seth, and others (2024). Measuring the Emissions and Energy Footprint of the ICT Sector: Implications for Climate Action (English). Washington, D.C.: World Bank. Available at http://documents.worldbank.org/curated/en/099121223165540890/P17859712a98880541a4b71d5787 6048abb

World Bank (2024). Green Digital Transformation: How to Sustainably Close the Digital Divide and Harness Digital Tools for Climate Action. Washington, D.C.

Contributing Partners

Gwangju Institute of Science and Technology (GIST) is a globally recognized South Korean institution specializing in science and technology education and research. The institution focuses on creating social and economic value through advancements in science and technology. GIST contributes to solving global challenges and establishing a scientific foundation for a sustainable future through innovative research and education. Notably, GIST plays a leading role in various fields such as environmental protection, energy conservation, and advanced technology development. Recently, GIST established the AIX School (AI Policy & Strategy Graduate School) and declared the HELP vision (Human-centric, Ethical Decision-making, Leadership & Innovation, and Problem-solving), aiming to contribute to human society through AI.

Contributor: Duk-Jo Kong

The GSMA is a global organisation unifying the mobile ecosystem to discover, develop and deliver innovation foundational to positive business environments and societal change. Our vision is to unlock the full power of connectivity so that people, industry, and society thrive. Representing mobile operators and organisations across the mobile ecosystem and adjacent industries, the GSMA delivers for its members across three broad pillars: Connectivity for Good, Industry Services and Solutions, and Outreach. This activity includes advancing policy, tackling today's biggest societal challenges, underpinning the technology and interoperability that make mobile work, and providing the world's largest platform to convene the mobile ecosystem at the MWC and M360 series of events. Find out more at www.gsma.com

Contributor: Leila Guici

Founded in 1987, Huawei is a leading global provider of information and communications technology (ICT) infrastructure and smart devices. We have 207,000 employees and operate in over 170 countries and regions, serving more than three billion people around the world. We are committed to bringing digital to every person, home and organization for a fully connected, intelligent world. Towards a digital and intelligent world, Huawei is integrating digital and power electronics technologies, developing clean power, and enabling energy digitalization to drive energy revolution for a better, greener future.

Korea Minting, Security Printing & ID Card Operating Corporation (KOMSCO), a state-owned enterprise established in 1951, has been exclusively producing and supplying specialized security products such as currency, e-passports, and national ID cards for 74 years in Korea. Recently, KOMSCO has expanded its business scope by promoting digital transformation with its accumulated technological expertise and experience in executing national projects. Designated by the Ministry of the Interior and Safety as the 'Specialized Agency for Mobile IDs,' KOMSCO currently operates a DID-based mobile ID platform and provides the mobile voucher service, a blockchain-based digital payment system, to support local economies.

Contributors: Yeonjoo Bang, Hyogeon Lee, Joonyong Park, and Jaesung Park

The Tony Blair Institute for Global Change (TBI) works with political leaders around the world to drive change. It is a not-for-profit organisation that provides expert advice on strategy, policy and delivery, unlocking the power of technology across all three. Its mission is to support leaders to build more open, inclusive and prosperous countries for people everywhere. TBI provides expertise in several sectors, including health care, agriculture transformation, climate and energy policy, and economic development, and works with a wide range of partners, including governments, bilateral and multilateral institutions, private corporations, academic institutions, foundations, and philanthropists who share its commitment and ambition.

Contributor: Kenddrick Chan

The United Nations Global Service Centre (UNGSC) is a leading provider of supply chain and digital technology services for the UN system. The Center works closely with clients and partners worldwide to develop and implement flexible, strategic, and responsible solutions. As part of the United Nations Department of Operational Support, Office of Supply Chain Management, UNGSC's optimized services constitute a lifeline in some of the world's most challenging locations.

Contributors: Michel Bergeron, Katharine Ghidella, Cynthia Primo Bou, Shamina de Gonzaga

The United Nations Climate Technology Center & Network (CTCN) is the implementation arm of the Technology Mechanism of the United Nations Framework Convention on Climate Change. The CTCN is hosted by the UN Environment Programme and headquartered in Copenhagen, Denmark. The CTCN promotes the accelerated development and transfer of climate technologies for energy-efficient, low-carbon and climate-resilient development, and mobilizes the expertise of a global network of about 800 civil society, finance, private sector, and research institutions to deliver technical assistance and capacity building at the request of developing countries.

Contributors: Woojin Han, Valentin Rudloff